HOW
TO MAKE A MAN HAPPY
A GUIDE FOR WOMEN

Denis Hickey

Trust is everything!

Published in 2019 by Vingdinger Publishing LLC
Copyright © Denis Hickey 2019

The moral right of the author has been asserted.

All rights reserved. No part of this publication may be reproduced or transmitted in any form or by any means, electronic or mechanical, including photocopy, recording, or any information storage and retrieval system, without permission in writing from the publisher.

ISBN: 978-0-9888588-8-6 (paperback)
ISBN: 978-0-9888588-7-9 (ebook)
Library of Congress Control Number: 2019904657

Front cover design and paperback formatting by Kazimierz Pelczar
Ebook formatting by Sun Editing & Book Design

Website: denishickey.com

Printed and bound in the USA

Acknowledgments

I would like to acknowledge my beautiful wife, Malgorzata, for making me happy. My daughters, Shannon and Chimene, and son Sean, make my life ultimately fulfilling as a dad. My mom, Kappy, grandmother Ahma, and aunts, Virginia and Jody, taught me respect for people in general, and as a result gave me the opportunity to be happy in my own skin. To Kathi Hickey for so many splendid shared years raising our girls. To Eric Joss and Jack Wiegardt for the quality of their lifelong friendship. To my editor, Jill Ronsley, thank you for your direction and skill in pairing my words and thoughts to say what I intend them to say (not an easy job), and to Kazimierz Pelczar, a philosopher himself, for your artwork and wise advice. Thanks to Frank Zolfo and Leszek Waniek for believing in me and providing thoughtful insights and stories. Finally, I would like to thank Barney Kierson for his thoughtful and insightful comments regarding the male and female interplay and Rich Rourke for his concise comments.

*Dedicated to Gil Holtzer,
my good friend and traveling buddy.*

About the Author

I grew up in a family headed by strong, loving women who provided me with admiration and appreciation for men. Those feelings were embellished with life experience gained over two long-lasting relationships that resulted in three well-balanced and delightful children. My working career reached top levels of business in Silicon Valley, and I was among few people to both build and fix companies on the leading edge of five distinct technologies.

In need of refurbishment, I retired early and backpacked for nine years to over 50 countries. My first year of travel is recounted in two non-fiction adventure novels (see below). During these travels, I engaged in discussion with hundreds of men and women, an experience supremely helpful in writing my companion series: *How to Make A Woman Happy* and *How to Make A Man Happy.*

I live in Poland, with my wife and son, pursuing my passions: writing, philosophy, family & friends, traveling, and a mellow satisfaction for life.

Other books by Denis Hickey, published
by Vingdinger Publishing:
The Breaking Free Series:
Breaking Free (Book 1)
The Traveler   (Book 2)
How To Make A Woman Happy

denishickey.com

Table of contents

INTRODUCTION 1

PART 1 DIFFERENCES BETWEEN MEN AND WOMEN . 10
   1. Why Know Men Better? 11
   2. How Humans Survived: Building the Brain 13
   3. Takeaways — Hunter/Gatherer..................... 25
   4. Differences That Define Us— General 33
   5. Differences That Define Us – Specific.............. 36
   6. Do Women "Get" Men?............................. 55

PART 2 HAPPY GUYS 66
   7. Raw Sex, Please 67
   8. Low Hanging Fruit 77
   9. Intimacy = Truth + Trust......................... 80
   10. Truth-Trust Conundrum.......................... 84
   11. HELP! Resolving Conflict 91
   12. Is Love a Secondhand Emotion? 96
   13. Weary Relationships 101
   14. Intimacy with Dads and Husbands 110
   15. Becoming a Woman Who Makes a Man Happy .. 124
   16. All You Need Is Trust 127

INTRODUCTION

Why publish a book about making men happy?

Because, simply stated, men deserve happiness, as do women. This is the second of my two-book series about how men and women can make each other happy. The first book, naturally, was *How to Make a Woman Happy.*

This book is organized into two parts with intriguing stories sprinkled throughout each chapter to illustrate different points. Although it's written for women, the smart guy can discover the why's of women and reset or modify a habit or two. Just as I did.

PART I: DIFFERENCES BETWEEN MEN AND WOMEN answers the question: Why know men better? I had a hard time writing the first part of this book. I started out with "men are simple creatures", but was met with a generally negative response in the male community, including me, probably because the concept is overused, trite and somewhat degrading. Men possess sophisticated genes that are built to have simple survival reactions. From an evolutionary standpoint, women had a more complex role in survival, obviously, because they carried the future in their bellies.

After a lot of hair-pulling about how to start this book, I realized I would have to begin at the beginning. How did human hunter-gatherers survive? It took millions of years for these imperfect creatures to morph into their modern version. Our hunter-gatherer nature thrust forward genes from generation to generation, upgrading them along the way until today. The pace of evolution may have speeded up during the last couple of hundred years, but my guess is that the effects of millions plays more heavily on the twenty-first century human than the effects of hundreds.

Men were built simply because the **fight, flight, or freeze** response needed to be reduced to fight or flight, an instantaneous survival reaction that controls how we men handle emotion, anger and fear. Those of you having intimate experience with males should recognize the fight or flight behavior when they are agitated. In any case, survival built our hunter-gatherer brains, and today we are left to noodle out how our genders can live closely together. **Part I** is devoted to understanding genetic differences between genders by exploring human survival and the role nature has played to draw men and women to each other and hold them together so that their young reach maturity.

Part I also provides takeaways on the hunter mentality. Discover for yourself the whys of his inclination to fix and solve, to take risks and to compete. Learn why and how his hunter brain is structurally simpler than her gatherer brain. Uncover the origin of his attitudes and inclinations towards communication, emotion, hierarchy, anger, commitment, freedom, alone-time, and, above all, sex.

I have come to realize how difficult it is for men and women to enjoy each other long-term if they don't sufficiently understand where their partner is coming from. In the past, and indeed today in less modern civilizations, this understanding was less important, because men hung out with men and women hung out with women. Modern society is more melded. If we want to make each other happy, we need to eliminate misunderstanding whenever possible by recognizing the impact of our male or female natures, our family culture and upbringing, our unique personalities, and, yes, even the time-frame within which each of us predominantly lives — past, present or future. If we also understand male and female brains and the chemicals that fuel them, we will possess the basis for more intimacy with each other.

INTRODUCTION

Take away this inescapable reality: if you had his genetic instructions and chemicals, you would act just like him. The same is true if you substitute "her" for "his/him." We evolved the way we are for good reason, plain and simple. Do you want to make a man happy? Understand that men think differently from women, just as surely as females have XX sex chromosomes and males have XY. That's fortunate, because being just the way we are has allowed humans to survive against all odds.

PART II: HAPPY GUYS points the way for you to:
- Improve your personal health and happiness by infusing your relationships with intimacy and trust.
- Feel better about yourself by adopting ideas discussed in Part II as catalysts for healing and self-discovery.
- Avoid genetic pitfalls that persist in our hunter-gatherer cave mentality, which are still at play in good as well as weary relationships.
- Grab the low-hanging-fruit of his happiness (described on these pages), and enjoy sweet intimacy with each bite.

Here's your chance to examine what it takes to make him happy — and yourself happy as a consequence, because your support makes him a better person. That's what this book strives to accomplish. Trust is the basis of success.

We can relax. The war of the sexes has been won. Really! The progress of female-male equality and social emancipation in much of the Western world over the last hundred years has been stupendous. What remains to be improved will happen. Think back 100 years. Women were second-class citizens. They required male pen names to write novels. They couldn't vote. They suffered through stifling male-oriented religions and social customs. They were often uneducated or educated to marry rather than to seek a fortune. "Their" fortune! Some countries prohibited (or continue to prohibit) women from inheriting. Think about how humiliating that would be—to depend on others because of unfair inheritance laws and underlying discrimination in education, and because your prospects for earning are limited or non-existent.

As a matter of principle and structure, none of those conditions exist in Western countries today. Sweden and the U.S. lead by example, with a third generation of gender equality, and other countries are following suit. Women are on their way to dominating. A woman's world. How great is that?

Despite the continuing fight to overcome unequal pay and glass ceilings, there is no arguing that in the US today, women dominate corporate middle management and most professions, such as law, banking, education, medicine, accounting, and human resources (which control salaries, by the way). The all-important industry of publishing written words is overwhelmingly controlled by women—from editors to agents to publishers to book reviewers to buyers—and women have surged to parity with men in writing bestsellers. Women have dominated music for the last 30 years with such megastars as J Lo, Beyoncé, Madonna, Whitney Houston, Christina Aguilera, Mariah Carey and older stars like Cher, Barbra Streisand, Tina Turner and so many others. In movies, during the 2017 Cannes Film Festival, for the first time, more women comprised juries than men, with Kate Blanchett holding the position of lead judge. Women have also staked their claim as action heroes. Go Angelina, Wonder Woman and Wonder Girl!

The list is growing, along with rewards and recognition. Western women don't need men to make their lives financially secure anymore. A basic structure that nourishes equality has been cemented into modern Western habits, and those habits are invading the rest of the world. Think of the media coverage and courts that are exposing violations of laws created to protect people from sexual harassment and discrimination; of the multinational corporations, like Hewlett Packard, that have spread policy internationally to protect their human resources from abuse; and, most importantly, of the 3rd generation of young men and women who grew up with equality as a given. Change may be hard for individuals, but, fundamentally, change is about a few adjustments on a regular basis that are implemented gradually.

Access to knowledge has changed, and as a consequence, 60% of American college graduates today are women versus a shallow 40% just 35 years ago. This evolution in education in such a short time ranks with the divorce rate increase of the twentieth century as one of the greatest anthropological changes ever.

In my book (pun intended), that's success.

True, only 5% of the Fortune 500 companies have female CEOs. That doesn't seem like much, but in time, if women want it, the glass ceiling will shatter too. Men have been entrenched as CEOs and Board members since business began, and "entrenched" is not easily replaced. Time and Numbers will determine the pace of change. Board members have already put 30 or so years of experience into the selection pool. Women have to serve the years in sufficient numbers for equality to take root. Helping the process along will be laws, such as that enacted by California, which mandates that companies in California also listed on major U.S. stock exchanges, have 1 to 3 female board members by the end of 2019.

Personally, I have mixed feelings about women trading family for glass ceiling participation. I like the equality aspect, but from a time perspective, most CEOs work horrendous hours. A friend who is the CEO of a small biotech company, for example, rolls out of bed at 5:30 in the morning to peruse emails and messages, arrives at work at 8:30, puts in a busy, often stressful day, and leaves at 7 p.m. for home unless he has a late evening meeting or frequent business dinner. Driving home he talks on the phone about business.

CEOs of most public corporations dedicate most of their mature existence to the organization. They are highly paid but probably not well-rounded people, because they have no time for what well-rounded requires. Take Fortune 500 CEO Gail Koziara Boudreau of Anthem Inc., for instance. According to Wikipedia, she is connected to 32 board members in three different organizations across 14 industries. Each industry has different business focuses with specific product lines, products and customers, thousands of employees to manage, buildings and equipment to rationalize and secure, agreements and major purchases to review and sign, new building locations to assess … Endless paperwork! Family time consists of squeezed-in vacations and maybe a free day during weekends.

So how does this current success of the female gender translate into a desire to make a man happy? Consider this: Men helped change culture to achieve gender equality. (Please hear me out.) The world may have seemed brutal at times over the last 10,000 years, but it's immensely better today than ever before. In much of the world, democracy is firmly entrenched, poverty is shrinking, entertainment is pervasive, intellectual pursuit is unfettered, science is rapidly shrinking the universe, and equality of genders is mostly achieved structurally—even while all of this continues to evolve and improve. That progress stems from the courage of countless men who fought and often died for a new order. Men are needed to help liberate women in many cultures that still make them second-class citizens.

INTRODUCTION

There you have it. Buried within that dialogue is the reason to make men happy. I am talking about the rank-and-file men and boys who are your friends, husbands, fathers, brothers, lovers, sons, nephews, cousins, support systems, providers and last, but certainly not to be considered lightly, soulmates. Sure, he's responsible for his own happiness. Thanks for pointing that out. But when he's happy, his incentive is to return the favor. Because every guy knows that if she's not happy, he won't be happy either. It's a two-way incentive.

Do women, in general, **trust** men enough to make them happy?

Let's not respond in haste. Let's take a moment to reflect. After all, buried in her genes are instances of ancestors defending against aggressive groups of men to protect themselves and their children, as well as fear of giving love to someone who betrays her trust.

During my travels, I visited Egypt's Valley of the Kings and marveled at five thousand-year-old drawings on earthen walls of various gods and goddesses. They were happy, sad, emotional, industrious and military. Significantly, both sexes worked together. Not far away as the crow flies, in Ephesus, Turkey, I witnessed more recent, but still ancient, artwork that depicted a single male god. Sure, there were women, but they played supporting roles. Naturally, I began to speculate about how civilization evolved—from the glorious Egyptians, who portrayed themselves through images depicting co-habitation of the sexes, to later societies who created often humorless, solitary male images of the likes of Jesus, Buddha and Mohammed.

My thinking evolved, through much deliberation, until the question arose, "Do women, in general, like men at all?" Consequently, during my extensive travels, I asked as many women as possible, "Do you like men?" My responders most often said "No!"

But when I changed this question to "What do you like about men?" the tone in the replies became soft and positive. Take, for example, the adventuress, Sweet Sue, who I met on a rust bucket steamer, traveling from a jungle on one of the Ssese Islands in Uganda to Kampala, the capital. Sue grinned longingly for several moments before answering thus: "I like men's looks and their ways of doing things. I like how they play. Men are adventuresome. They take risks. They really know how to stir up bloody hell! They surprise me. I like talking to men. They're insightful and gripping at times. I think men are more honest and straight forward than women. And I like the way they feel … you know—solid, tall and enveloping when they hug."

Other women said, "I like that they are reliable. I like their sense of humor and fun, and the way they make eye contact and smile at me. They make me feel safe. I like …" (sometimes with a husky voice) "… his muscles! I like men's companionship; they make terrific friends. I like their sense of 'we.' I like their intelligence and ability to make a decision. I like men's compatibility and the intimacy they provide. I like the sex. I like the power they project and the strong way they hold me. I like that they challenge and ask questions, and their sense of responsibility. I like that they spoil me."

That's about 30 attributes.

The upshot to me is that even women who don't like guys in general like the hell out of them *in particular.* How else do you explain unrestrained female mania manifested in hysterical behavior towards musicians like Coldplay, the late David Bowie, Justin Timberlake, Sting, or, going way back, Elvis, the Beatles, Sinatra or Bing Crosby? Wild screams and crying just to get a glimpse … or exchange one. What is that about?

INTRODUCTION

Could women live without the drama, passion and romance they have with men? Without the love and commitment depicted in the stories of Casablanca, Antony and Cleopatra, Romeo and Juliet, Sindbad The Sailor, The Titanic or Dr. Zhivago? Or in real life stories, for that matter—without a love that each woman dreams of in the secret reaches of her heart? Without songs that capture the hunger and urgency of love? Without men's almost hidden smiles? Without him saying "everything's going to be all right"? What would life be like without male gurus like Billy Graham, Buddha, Jesus, Mohammad, Jon Stewart, Joel Olsteen, Clint Eastwood, Denzel Washington or John Kennedy? Doesn't the very fiber of our bodies cry out at times for a soulmate to possess us in times of loneliness or triumph? How about that desperate need to touch him at the airport after a long absence? Or simply, that magnetic connection when he says, "Lying by your side is the greatest pleasure I've ever known?"

PART 1
DIFFERENCES...
BETWEEN MEN AND WOMEN

1. Why Know Men Better?

Because men and women click by nature. We are hooked on each other. Drugged! Addicted! Obsessed! Love-a-holics! Within the DNA of her extra X chromosome, and in every single one of the 40 trillion or so microscopic cells in her body, nature has embedded this clear message: Men are necessary for your survival. Neither men nor women would be born without the existence of both.

So, feel in your bones the need to understand men and make them happy.

Despite the cliché, "men are simple creatures," they complicate, seem unfathomable, act contrary and, at times, they are dangerous. They elicit complex questions like:

- Why can't he commit?
- Why can't he express his feelings?
- Why does he need to fix me?
- Why is sex the only thing he thinks about?
- How can I be the one?

Understand him better and these questions go away. With understanding comes empathy, respect and, eventually, trust—the greatest of all virtues. Men need understanding, especially now, when male college graduation rates and employment levels are severely on the decline, and sharp minds and communication skills are rendering brawn obsolete. Today's employment and graduation statistics and websites offering men any kind of sex they want should be alarming for women who want to relate, love or marry.

Here's why:

Rapidly decreasing qualified men in your "Eligible Male Pool" results in increased competition from other women for fewer desirable mates.

Captivating and keeping the right guy today requires a sophisticated understanding of this creature and his needs. This book begins with reference to a time millions of years ago, when humans struggled to survive without long teeth, a heavy body, the ability to run fast or the physique to climb with agility. It is directed at women who desire blue-chip relationships with men. It assumes, and I believe proves, this premise:

Hunter-gatherer genes developed over millions of years dominate our lives today!

This is nothing radically new. But to skeptics—to those who disdain the hunter-gather concept and the validity of the premise in this age of artificial intelligence, microprocessors and drastically changing female dominance—I challenge you to read this book.

Why know men better? "Because the greatest thing you'll ever learn is to love and be loved in return." (The movie "Moulin Rouge")

2. How Humans Survived: Building the Brain

Humans have adapted to dominate their environment. Ants have too, but they can't build New York City or construct a spaceship. Consider this nugget of biology with respect to Homo Sapiens: After conception, precisely when our embryo was formed, two sets (or pairs) of 23 chromosomes, one set from our mother and one set from our father (46 chromosomes in all), joined together, and we instantly possessed, in each of the 40 trillion cells in our body (scientists estimate between 30 and 50 trillion), genetic qualities of hunter and gatherer—qualities honed by our ancestors over millions of years.

In the 23rd pair, human females have two X chromosomes and males have an XY pairing. Whether a person has XX or XY is determined when a sperm fertilizes an egg, creating a fertilized ovum. Male donors determine the embryo's sex. Specifically, the 23rd chromosome our father passed on to us determined our sex. If he passed on an "X" chromosome a person is a girl. If he passed on a "Y" a person is a boy.

Of course, nature makes exceptions and fiddles with the process. Although there appears to be a faint indication that chromosomes play a part in homosexual development, that is not my focus. Besides, making men happy is not gender specific.

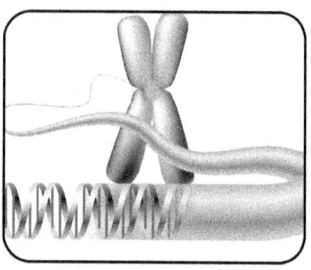

Chromosomes are thread-like molecules made of protein and one molecule of DNA. Genes are stored in DNA.

Passed from generation to generation, chromosomes contain inherited genetic instructions. Chromosomes are thread-like molecules made of protein and a DNA molecule. Genes, which are stored in the DNA, reach a very long way back in time. Males pass on a Y chromosome approximately 50% of the time, which is nature's way of ensuring that approximately the same number of males and females are born.

23 sets of chromosomes in each cell of your body
US National Library of Medicine

The image above is that of a male because of the Y chromosome in the bottom right 23rd set. A female would have a second "X" roughly six times larger than the guy's Y, with more than a thousand additional genes and millions more DNA instructions. A guy's Y contains only 26 genes: 16 for cell maintenance, nine for sperm production and one gene responsible for male sexual traits and indirectly triggering development of male sexual organs.

According to Natalie Angier in her book, **Woman,** the genes in a female's second X are sitting around doing nothing. But subsequent science has shown a significant portion to be active. My theory is that genes in the second X act like parallel computers that keep programs running when something goes wrong with the main processor. Nature doesn't build anything without a reason. Perhaps genes in this second X contain a lot of subliminal programming on how to deal with males or take care of chores males are incapable of or ill prepared for, like shopping and talking. Keep this second X genetic treasure chest in mind as we go along. Genes harbor an unimaginable amount of data and instructions. Some 155 million DNA building blocks, 5% of the total DNA in the body's cells, reside in an X chromosome. It makes me wonder what information she's getting that we guys are not.

My take is that the female has an awful lot of discussion going on in her genes, while the guy is fixated on fixing problems in his trillions of cells. I'll also bet the guy's Y contains little or nothing to direct him on how to understand a woman. (You can get those instructions from my book, **How to Make a Woman Happy,** which has a complete set of instructions.)

Building the Human Brain

Many would argue that Homo Sapiens survived because of their powerful brain. But the advantages built into the large human cortex, compared to those in the brains of other land species, were developed by family Hominidae over millions of years, before the relatively recent Cognitive Revolution (estimated to have begun around 70,000 years ago)—which, according to Yuval Harari's book, Sapiens: *A Brief History of Humankind,* jumpstarted the human brain to achieve wondrous things. Clearly, our brain evolved gradually to launch us into the Cognitive Revolution. How did we survive until then? Again, we weren't as fast, nimble, clawed or toothy as the other guys, by far! However, we did have two attributes that other species didn't have: a hand with five fingers and a superior ability to mate. Could these have assured survival for all those years the human cortex waited to be fully activated? Let's let our minds wander in that direction.

Hands.

*Story: During the early years of Apple Computer, in the late 70s, when the manufacture of microcomputers, as they were called then, was considered **leading edge**, I was engaged in a conversation with Mike Watts, the CEO of our microcomputer company, Dynobyte, now a Silicon Valley museum piece. On the leading edge it's common to talk about the evolution of technology or how it might be used in the future. This particular discussion concerned the evolution of the human brain. Mike felt that the greatest contribution* to development of the brain was hands, while I posited it was human sexual habits.

"Move your fingers around," Mike suggested. "Grab this pen. Toss it in the air." (Try this yourself.) "Notice your thumb—a wonderful addition, don't you think? Now feel the skin on your wrist. Notice the sensitivity in the tips of your fingers as they stroke. How does it feel? The brainpower necessary to manipulate hands to their fullest is staggering. I would have to put a microprocessor in every joint to get the hand to move each finger the way the human brain does. And today's microprocessors and memory systems are years away from what I could hope to achieve. Hands are cool!"

"You have a good point," I said, flexing my fingers. "At the same time, to survive alongside species that were physically superior, humans needed to produce lots of offspring and keep them alive. They needed a dominant reproductive desire and capability. Human females can mate any time of the year, even during pregnancy. She has the potential to be pregnant constantly. No other mammals I know of can duplicate that." I pointed my finger at him. "This advantage allowed us to produce enough offspring for survival. It's the old sea turtle theory," I concluded. "If you can't out-fight them, out-produce them."

Mike considered for a moment, massaged his hands, a roguish smile creasing his face. "Think about how useful hands are in lovemaking," he finally said. "How the very act of touching your mate's skin stirs tingles of passion in both of you. And hands are no less efficient for hunting and gathering.

"Let's end this discussion this way," he concluded. "Hands and sexual prowess are clearly connected to building the cortex."

Appraise for yourself Dr. Wilder Penfield's homunculus (below). It demonstrates metaphorically how the body is represented in our cortex. Check how much of the cortex and its associated neurons are used just to manipulate hands compared to other body parts. Only our lips and tongue, used for tasting, eating and sex, are in the same ballpark.

"This homunculus" shows how the body is represented in the cortex. The biggest features, such as the hands, have the most neurons.

Superior ability to mate.

According to Joe Quirk, author of ***Sperm Are from Men, Eggs Are from Women,*** "The one true thing you can say about every single one of your billions of ancestors is that they each reproduce. In the race to reproduce only the best reproducers won, every generation. Think of that. The most powerful force in our bodies and brains is the accumulated desire of all our ancestors, refined, concentrated, and made more powerful than any desire we imagine more important. With such a horny force animating every microscopic detail of our cells, we should think of all human needs as sub-needs arising from the desire to procreate. Our hunger for love, our ambitions, our desire to belong, our urge to make beautiful things, our need to talk, our voracious curiosity, our fear of death, our longing for transcendence, our willingness to die for our community, our ache for God. All our qualities evolved to the extent that they serve the reproduction of genes in ourselves and our beloved annoying relatives."

Chew on Quirk's statement: *We should think of all human needs as sub-needs arising from the desire to procreate.*

Over the two million years of being the Homo Erectus species, chromosomes loaded with genes, DNA, mysterious instructions and contemporary reproductive experience were passed along from generation to generation, through centuries and millennia, until finally, they reached you. That's at least 130,000 generations of procreative improvement loaded into every cell in your body, with each cell containing an exact copy of all 46 chromosomes. Think of all your ancestors, each with distinct and inherited talents and powers that translated into leaders, nice guys, powerful women, nurturing individuals or the black sheep of evolution. Think of all the mothers who gave strength to our genes. Nature preprogramed every one of our 40 trillion cells with ferocity, sensitivity and procreative desire. Why?

Oxford biologist Richard Dawkins posits, "The basic unit of evolution is not the individual organism, but genes. Individuals are born, live and die, but genes live forever through reproduction." Reproduction! We could quote Samuel Butler's famous aphorism, "a hen is only an egg's way of making another egg," and say by extension that a human is only "a gene's way to produce another gene".

Maybe nature in its vast wisdom wanted sexual desire in humans to be so predetermined, so hardwired, that every cell in us cries in a glorious crescendo: **All human needs are sub-needs that arise from the predominant desire to procreate.** There is more, of course, like what are these genetic messages doing after birth? Let's face it: human babies are not like gazelles who hit the ground running to avoid hungry predators. To survive in the world alongside such predators, human babies and their genes needed time to develop after birth. They needed their mom, food and protection. They particularly needed mom to bond with a guy, or guys, for at least six years, or until they could fend for themselves. Guys were not only programmed to spread seed. I mean, creation was easy and delightful—to the max even—but survival was another matter. Which leads us to … bonding!

Nature came up with ways to create this phenomenon of bonding so that humans could move up the food chain. My theory, and I'm sure others have had the same thought, is that two forces would stimulate enough desire for a couple (or a few members of the clan) to bond for six or so years, until a child could fend for himself or herself. Let's call these two forces attraction-of-opposites and chemical inducement.

The attraction-of-opposites is a natural force in the universe. When opposites attract in humans, with survival at stake, a couple have more options in their survival tool-kit than like personalities have. This makes sense. Opposites have different talents, whereas likes have similar talents. The more talents there are in the combined kit, the better the chance of survival. Attraction of opposites is an invisible force behind our selection of partners and friends. Attracted to an opposite, a meticulous woman falls in love with a carefree traveler, a princess falls in love with a commoner. Goody-Two-Shoes might pursue the meanest dude in the clan! Savers are attracted to throw-it-awayers.

Electrically charged objects, which contain more protons than electrons, are positively charged. Objects that contain fewer protons than electrons are negatively charged. Oppositely charged doodads exert an attractive influence upon each other. They need each other. In contrast, two objects with a similar charge repel each other.

In the world of static electricity

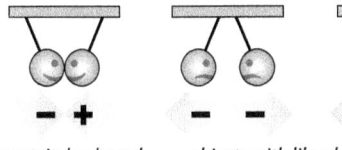

oppositely-chrged objects attract

objects with like charges repel

(Flickr Physics Photo)

God forbid that savers, for instance, should be attracted to each other! When I lived in Orinda, California, our house was on a hill, and at the bottom was a house with a three-car garage. But no car could fit inside and the door was permanently open to nature—because it was full of floor-to-ceiling stuff. The result of likes attracting.

Chemical inducement. This bonding force may have snared a cave-dwelling big lug or two out of their bachelor pads long enough to keep the family fed and competitive within the clan. Enhancing the primary seducers, estrogen and testosterone, pheromones and other love chemicals like oxytocin and dopamine (which create the sense of bonding and relationship) and PeA (similar to the drug, ecstasy) are said to promote feelings of infatuation, excitement and euphoria when that special someone enters the picture. Osmology, the science of the sense of smell, has determined that men and women are attracted to each other through arousal-stimulating pheromones, which signal sexual desire, fertility and deep emotions. Pheromones, primarily perceived through olfactory sensors, are excreted in several parts of the body including skin, sweat glands, saliva and urine. When humans secrete these minuscule chemical messengers, they are subconsciously detected by another's nose, brain and nervous system.

Researchers say saliva contains molecules from all glands and organs in the body. So one delicious kiss and your bodies are checking out each others chemicals, health and genes for compatibility. One kiss and millions of cells are running around searching. Ooh Lala if there is a match! That's some kind of cellular machine!

Originally, the bond needed to last many years for offspring and mother to avoid having to go it alone in difficult environments. These days, if you want to live harmoniously after the pheromone addiction lapses (two to four years)—and the opposite becomes annoying—you might pay heed to Charles Darwin's observation: *"It is not the strongest of the species that survives, nor the most intelligent… It is the one that is most adaptable to change."*

About Hunters and Gatherers

On average, men are bigger than women, with a 10 to 15% larger brain mass. The larger brain evolved due to the relative size of its host, and possibly from the risks inherent in hunting or exploring new lands for habitation. Hunters rely on hand signals, minimal discussion and lots of risk. They communicate primarily using the left side of the brain, which governs logic and tasks. This explains why guys have a less developed sense of emotion. If some beast, its mouth dripping blood, just killed your buddy and now stood staring menacingly at you, there would be little time for emotion if you wanted to save yourself.

Our hunter of yesteryear was probably not your man around the house. He had two and a half times more brain space devoted to sexual drive and aggression than a woman, and testosterone made him less communicative. Picture him coming home with a deer slung over his shoulder. Tired. On edge. He hangs around for a couple of days. Has sex. Does a few chores around the cave like decorating the wall with a hand painting, cleaning discarded bones off the floor and fixing the boulder at the entrance. After a few days, he gets off his bed of branches and brush and grunts, "Hunt … now!"

Gatherers, on the other hand, were constructed to communicate. This makes sense because of their foraging for berries, caring for children and participation in complicated communal work. They are blessed with a complex, tightly woven brain mass and strong communication genes in both their left and right brains, the right being associated with cognitive skills like creativity, emotion and intuitiveness. In fact they have 11% more brain centers for language and hearing than men. Nature designed them and waited until now—the dawn of woman's world, when muscles are for looks and communication is paramount—to fully utilize the talents inherent in gatherer genes.

So shall it be written; so shall it be done!

Quirk believes that to understand each other we must understand our hunter-gatherer sexual natures. "Males have facial hair, females have oversized breasts," he says. "Males have oversized penises. Females have exaggerated waist-to-hip ratios. Women are better at keeping track of many things in space. Men are better able to turn shapes around in their minds and still recognize them. Again, because women gathered and men hunted." Personally, I have always found women to have an attractive dark side which I believe is inherited from ancient gatherers. The looks, the moans, the ecstasy, the passion that only women possess drives guys wild. Pure, unadulterated fun, and the best part for us guys is that all of this satisfies the needs inherent in survival of the fittest.

Survival of the species is the dominant driver of humans. When the chromosome identifies male or female in the fetus, powerful hunting or gathering forces activate in the genes. Those forces continue to evolve to fit modern life, but in the grand scheme of things, genes that tell us what to do have been evolving, and I mean this in an intertwined biological and social sense, over a few million years for the human genus. The pace of evolution may have accelerated during the last thousand years, but my guess is that the effects of millions of years has not been changed significantly by the last few hundred.

My point is that men and women act the way they do because we humans evolved that way, plain and simple. Our day-to-day is printed in our genes. That's who we are! To make men happy, I believe it's crucial to understand that men think differently from how women think, just as surely as females have XX and males XY.

3. Takeaways — Hunter/Gatherer

What to take away about men from all this biology

- **On Hunting.** The job — create, protect and provide. Hunter characteristics to do this job: precise language, independence, strategy, game playing, bring home food. Sound familiar? Today's homo sapien male has a job which is an end in itself. He brings home money to put food on the table. Money and responsibility are intertwined in the modern hunter. His muscles are of little use now, except for show and sports, and he likes guns.
- **On Risk Taking.** It takes courage to ask for a date or a kiss? I distinctly remember the first time I went to the movies with a girl, maneuvering my arm gingerly and secretively along the top of her seat, aiming for her distant shoulder and cringing at the prospect of rejection. As equality's roots dig deeper, will females need to assume this risk?
- **On Competition.** Competition and aggression are hardwired in most boys. When he matures, work and protecting family take the place of sports, and money becomes the score. **His greatest fear: running out of money!**
- **On Simplicity.** His brain is sophisticated but built modestly, with considerably fewer but precise instructions. For instance, he knows instinctively which way to turn a nut on a bolt.
- **On alone Time.** Hunting is quiet, often lonely. It offers an element of freedom and an escape from confrontation

with others, male or female. Being alone is also an escape from expectations. He relaxes around the cave after a tough day in the forest, but there's always cave-work to be done, and expectations. Ugh! He's only got 26 genes in the 23rd chromosome, and none of those 26 seem to address her expectations. Finally, the hairy brute picks himself off the dirt floor and goes hunting with his buddy.

- **On Communication.** The hunter points and flashes fingers to communicate where and how many. He's direct, concise and to the point. He uses only one or two measured words to say anything. Discussion means risk of attack or loss of prey. Today, the average male phone conversation lasts 30 seconds.
- **On Emotion.** It's 150,000 years ago. Your buddy was just killed by a large beast. No time to emote. Decide: Fight! Flee!

Men are likely to be unemotional, a characteristic modern society often tries to change. What makes more sense during an attack by a deadly force, an emotional response or stifling emotions to deal with whatever is after you? In the movie *Six Days Seven Nights*, with pirates chasing them, an emotional *Robin Monroe* (Anne Heche) says to cantankerous pilot, Quinn Harris (Harrison Ford), that when running from pirates a woman wants her man to be "mean and armed!"

Story: *Following a variety of misadventures while traveling from India to Katmandu, our supremely crowded bus took a brisk right turn and struck an old man crossing the street. Through the window, I saw his half-clad body fly through the air and heard*

PART 1 DIFFERENCES *3. Takeaways — Hunter/Gatherer*

the thud as he landed. The bus carried a full load of passengers, with a crowd standing in the aisle. The poor fellow was killed on impact.

Instead of stopping and seeing to the old man, the diminutive driver halted the bus briefly to confer with his on-board money collector. Then the driver resumed his seat and pushed the pedal to the metal to get away. Female travelers in the front of the bus were in tears.

Sitting four rows back, I watched two thoughts rattle my brain. Should I tell the driver to stop, knowing from experience that in parts of Africa and India stopping often meant instant deadly justice by locals to the driver and possibly the passengers? The second thought was a wish that I could feel the same grief that the women felt, who, through their tears, mourned the old man but also left this critical decision to guys.

In short order, we were stopped by a carload of local men who emptied onto the street, ready to avenge the deceased. At the same time, a police car appeared. A composed officer exited his vehicle and slowly approached the bewildered, nervous bus driver. They exchanged a few words, and the policeman ushered the bus driver into the rear of the police car. With everyone looking on but not interfering, a second officer emerged from the shotgun seat and walked slowly and unobtrusively to the door of the bus, as if the scene was commonplace. He climbed onto the vacant driver's seat, slid behind the wheel and drove us four miles to a grassy field behind a schoolhouse, where we disembarked. The police assured the travelers that other buses to Kathmandu would be along shortly to deliver us to our various destinations. No names or addresses were taken, and no statements of what happened were procured. At the schoolhouse, the locals who had been on our bus seemed to split seamlessly from the scene.

Another bus arrived, and for six hours I rode to Kathmandu on the roof along with a contingent from Israel. I never knew what arrangements had been made for our passage. Sitting comfortably on top of baggage, I marveled at the emerald beauty of the mountains, the slat bridges across deep canyons sculpted by raging rivers, the sun nudging below a pink, deep red and sky-blue sunset, kids sitting on a low fence bordering a high cliff talking and shitting together, and locals at pit-stops selling and tossing food up to us on the roof. Occasionally we climbed down to push our bus as we navigated onerous bends in the dusty, narrow, rut-strewn road. Back on the roof, my mind was consumed by thoughts of where to jump if the bus were to careen off the road and fall over a cliff, only to tumble down and down and—!

Survival and new adventure pushed the thought of the old man's death and the emoting women far from the front of my mind. **But I have no illusions that we humans evolved to create a gender balance between emoting and fixing, and if we want harmony, that we should respect these diverse activities.**

- **<u>On hierarchy.</u>** At every party I threw or attended, discussion groups started as a mix of men and women. An hour later groups were divided by gender. The more important men dominated male discussions. Chain of command. Men don't like being ordered around or led by equals.
- **<u>On Anger.</u>** Returning to 150,000 years ago, our hunter takes a few moments to absorb how his buddy got eaten by the beast. Meanwhile, hormones are filling his brain, reducing his fear and making him angry and aggressive— enough to take revenge! Hormones work to protect his family from threats when they are in danger. Scientists say the area in his brain for suppressing anger is smaller than the same area in the female brain. That's why anger is more common for men than women. But as he ages, the ratio of estrogen to testosterone increases and he mellows. That would be me now.

- **On men's inclination to fix and solve problems.**
  Louann Brizendine, M.D., says in her national best-selling book, *The Female Brain*, "… when faced with a loved one's emotional distress, the part of his brain built for problem solving and fixing situations will immediately spark. In her companion book, *The Male Brain*, she dubs the male brain "a lean, mean problem-solving machine."

Nature drives hunters to solve, fix and move on (remember the fixing that goes on in his Y chromosome). If you want someone to listen, empathize with drama, sympathize or soothe, choose a gatherer. This makes sense, doesn't it? Hunters can't afford to have the same thing go wrong twice. They need to confront and fix so that it doesn't happen again. To fix something, gatherers often needed concurrence from other gatherers in the clan, which requires tact and diplomacy, rather than confrontation and confidence skills. Guys fix and solve.

Hint: If you want him to do something, give that big lug a list to complete in his own way and at his own pace. Lists work better than constant reminders.

- **On sex.** Grass is green. Men want sex. Genes! Evolution! Survival of the fittest! Passing on genes is his destiny, his number one job and passion. Brizendine also says in *The Female Brain*, "Men have on average 10 to 100 times more testosterone than women … Just as women have an eight-lane superhighway for processing emotions while men have a small country road, men have O'Hare Airport as a hub for processing thoughts about sex whereas women have the airfield nearby that lands small and private planes."
- **On commitment.** For early humans to survive, hunters supported pregnant females and those with children long enough for their offspring to mature.

- **On freedom.** Freedom nags at men. The opposite of oppression, freedom is the noble quest. "Fight for our freedom, boys!" Freedom is also living in the moment, with no responsibility for anyone or anything but ones self—the hunter in us, perhaps. A dichotomy occurs when men work and raise a family. His noble quest, however, was often a double-edged sword for women. The freedom he fought for often took his life. To many women, that meant abandonment—she lost a husband and the father of her kids, putting the family's very survival at risk. Today, freedom, in all senses, is attainable by both genders.

*Story: I just finished reading the bestseller, **Nothing to Lose**, featuring the tough but fair hero, Jack Reacher (played by Tom Cruise in the movie, **Never Go Back**). The author, Lee Child, has written 20 other Reacher thrillers, and apparently one of his books is sold every 20 seconds. The front cover of **Nothing to Lose** shows a lone guy walking down the deserted main street of a small Colorado town at sunrise. He has only the clothes on his back and the shoes on his feet, and in his pockets is nothing but paper money, an expired passport, an ATM card and a clip-together toothbrush.*

Reacher tips the scales at 250 pounds. He has no job, no address and no baggage, but he does have a monthly army pension. He travels by bus or hitch hikes, and when he can't find rides, he walks. Reacher never turns back. All he wants for breakfast is a cup of coffee and steak and eggs. He's a tough-as-nails loner whose curiosity matches his passion for sex, but he has no long-term relationships. That's freedom! When his clothes start to smell, he buys new ones at a janitorial supply store at reasonable prices. Perfect! His hair is short

and tidy, he shaves in the morning and his fly is zipped. Awesome!
About Reacher, *famous readers have said the following:*

Patricia Cornwell: *"Sometimes you just want someone who can beat the S… out of people. I pick up Jack Reacher when I'm in the mood for someone big to solve my problems."*

Karin Slaughter: *"One of the sexiest characters in fiction."*
Ken Folett: *"Reacher grabs me on page 1 and never lets go."*
Stephen King: *"The coolest continuing series character."*
Lucy Mangan: *"I am very much in love with Jack Reacher—as a man and role model. If I can't shag him, I want to be him."*

Heavy. But that's freedom for you. I was free for several years, traveling the world, with no responsibility for anyone but myself. I was only responsible for finding someplace to eat, sleep and relieve myself. I wouldn't want freedom all the time, but it's nice to have the experience.

What about freedom for a guy who doesn't travel? How about sports? Now, that's a form of noble quest!

Story: *A female lawyer I knew said, "Denis, what is it that you men love about football? I don't get football!"*

I asked whether she liked ballet. She said, "Yes."

"Well, football pits an immense, ferocious offensive line of heavy muscular men against another savage defensive line of heavy muscular men who are trying to crash through the offensive line to stop an odd-shaped football from progressing. The task of the defensive line is to seek out and destroy whoever has the ball. On offense, the quarterback, knowing he may get pounced upon, pummeled and obliterated, fades back for space behind his protective offensive line and launches, over a swirling brutal mass, a perfect spiral into the

air. The ball's assignment: to be caught by the right player far downfield. As the football spins with perfect symmetry, further and further, whether in bright sunshine or on a snowy day, a wide receiver is running as fast as his long legs will carry him, his eyes riveted on the ball, all the while trying to elude defenders intent on grabbing that same football or on otherwise distracting him viciously. At the very last moment, the wide receiver launches into a high jump, like a ballerina's pirouette, and in one magical instant stretches his pliant hands up in the air to corral the spinning ball perfectly into his soft but firm flesh. Having snared the ball, he pulls the pigskin firmly to his chest. What could be more aesthetically satisfying?"

She said, "Yeah, but how can you watch football for three hours?"

Do one thing for your hunter — your dad, boyfriend, grandfather, uncle, brother or friend.

One thing you know his hunter instincts will appreciate. One thing can't be hard to do, right? Know something about his favorite sport, enough to converse with him for one minute. Say something like "Wow, that Curry's got a sweet shot!" (He'll give you the athlete's name.) "Is he for real? Incredible!"

How hard is that? Better yet, buy tickets and join him at the game. Guys love company watching sports. Can't stand sports? Give him your blessing to go off to the game with his buddies. Give him "Reacher time"!

4. Differences That Define Us — General

"I say banaaanas and you say bananas. I say po-taaatas and you say potatoes …"

Do we really understand each other? It's hit and miss, I'd say. Understanding and recognizing differences between people provides a solid basis for figuring out who they are and whether we can trust them. Understanding is key to everyone.

Did you know intelligence in humans can be determined by the number of differences we perceive, the number of shades of gray, so to speak? The greater the number of differences perceived, the greater the intelligence and the easier it is to understand someone. Let's glance at levels of differences that Tanya, a potential house buyer, might perceive during a tour of a house and her discussion with the owners, Halim and Karma, who want to sell.

Base level. Tanya notices that Halim's clothes are neat, his shoes are shined, he wears an oversized sweatshirt and he speaks with a slight foreign accent. **Perception:** He's a strangely dressed foreigner.

Next level. Tanya observes that tools and doodads are impeccably stored on hooks on the garage wall, that Karma's car in the driveway is dusty and full of candy wrappers, and the house is neat and tidy. **Perception:** They are both neat. He's a perfectionist. She doesn't care much about cars.

Higher level. Tanya notices during the conversation that Halim speaks precisely but avoids any hint of personal interest in her, and Karma speaks erratically but asks penetrating questions that she doesn't follow up. **Perception:** Halim is self-absorbed and Karma has a short attention span.

Deeper level (snoopy). Tanya uses carefully constructed questions to learn that Halim manages a hardware store, works late and doesn't interact with the family when he returns home (gleaned during a slight tiff between him and Karma in the kitchen). She notices that the large kitchen is cluttered with pictures of kids and displays a great set of pots and pans. Asking disarming questions during a timely silence, Tanya elicits from Karma that Halim is cranky in the morning, she quits work promptly at 5 p.m. to pick up their 13-year-old daughter, and she goes to dinner with friends twice a week to maintain her sanity, while Halim chimes in that he cooks. **Perception:** Their words and body language signal that sale of the house might be court-ordered or due to an impending divorce, and Tanya is in a good negotiating position.

Higher and deeper. Tanya learns while scanning the 13-year-old daughter's room that the girl is bulimic and her father hasn't touched her in years because, as he explains after a verbal prod from Karma, when she was five years old the daughter indicated she didn't like touch. His 23-year-old daughter is separated from her husband because she can't make him happy but is trying to reconcile with him because she recently purchased a book by Denis Hickey on how to make a man happy. **Perception:** Halim is out of touch and in serious need of female support and intimacy, and the oldest daughter has good taste in *how-to* books.

Differences paint a picture. Higher levels of understanding, and therefore intelligence (or intel if you prefer), are accompanied by curiosity and the ability to ask risky questions diplomatically. Perceiving differences is a function of three things: observation, a detective-like curiosity and questions. Questions can be fine-tuned with practice … practice…!

Story: *In the movie* **Yentl,** *Barbra Streisand impersonates a male student named Anshel (the name of her deceased brother) to gain acceptance at the local yeshiva. At a time when Jewish women were not allowed to study the Talmud and Torah, or read books for that matter, Streisand's character is interviewed by the dean of the school. Flustered at the end of the interview, the disguised student apologizes for asking so many questions instead of impressing the dean with knowledge. The kindly and wise teacher responds, "He asks a lot of questions, this one … It is by their questions that we choose our students, not only by their answers. Your father taught you well, Anshel."*

What Works for Guys

***Understand differences
between you and him.
Remember to ask questions,
because love is an exploration.***

5. Differences That Define Us – Specific

Recognizing differences between you and him often eliminates misunderstanding. Let's look at four categories of differences that I believe predominantly impact understanding anyone:
1. family culture and upbringing
2. our male or female nature
3. our unique personality
4. time frame a person predominantly lives in: past, present or future

Family Culture and Upbringing

The family I grew up in yelled and argued to make a point. **Result:** I have a conflict-oriented personality with the potential to be cool or volatile. My wife, on the other hand, comes from a family that could not bear conflict. Their disagreements were short-lived: Why suffer the pain of talking issues out? **Result:** Longer-life conflict issues.

Story: *I met Sweet Sue traveling in Luxor, Egypt, during a backpack trip around the world. We spent several days discovering the mysteries of the Temple of Karnak, exploring its decayed columns and pylons and listening to the whispers of its ancient pha-*

raohs. A couple of years later, Sue drove from San Francisco to visit me in northern California's Santa Cruz Mountains. We walked along a forest stream discussing her impending engagement, while listening to the tweets of flittering robins and bluebirds and the trickle of water flowing down and around a rocky floor. She needed a friend in whom to confide her discomfort with the thought of living forever with her partner, who was so different from her.

"Have you discussed the differences?" I asked.

"No. Real issues are difficult to discuss," she said. "I know about Michael's family. His parents were dictatorial, and he has a major problem with his father. My family was easy-going—we discussed a variety of subjects at dinner and handled our conflicts without anger. But I'm worried about how we will raise our children and what philosophy will be acceptable for both of us."

"And your love for him?"

"Oh, I'm madly in love with him."

"Have you discussed his family's way of doing things and the differences in your family cultures?" I asked.

She looked at her feet as she replied. "I feel negligent about that. But it's not romantic and I hesitate to spoil our moods."

"Wasn't it Carl Jung who said, 'Until you make the unconscious conscious, it will direct your life, and you will call it fate'?"

"Jung's unconscious probably directed his life," she said sarcastically. "But existence is 90% subconscious, right? So, I get his point. Issues will remain until we address them—which will probably be after we're married." She looked at me with concern in her eyes. "Maybe I'll be too easy and pliable because my dad was easy."

"For what it's worth," I said, "I didn't have much success adjusting to my wife's family culture. It was an improvement in many ways. Still …"

"Reality. Right!" she said with a shrug. "Being in love and making the subconscious conscious by not marrying because of your partner's family habits would be like getting off crystal meth. Love is an addiction."

Family culture lies submerged within our personality. As years pass cultural habits rise to the surface as if sprouting from deep genetic seeds. Look around you. Check out how many people slowly begin to resemble their parents.

Story: *I was jealous of my friend's lunches. He grew up with his grandmother and mother, both of whom tended to his needs. My mom had five kids in four years and worked as a nurse. I made my own sandwiches for lunch: mostly original peanut butter and grape jelly. The jelly seeped into my brown carrying bags, imprinting embarrassing dark purple on the outside.*

His mother and grandmother made great sandwiches. Of course, they added a banana and cookies to their darling's spotless, smooth bag. When we were teenagers, we would drive to our summer beach jobs on Long Island, and sometimes he shared his lunch of the day. My favorite was chopped ham sandwiches. It was not lost on me later in life that each of his four children, two daughters and two sons, grew up and raised families in which the two daughters and two daughters-in-law, who'd held good jobs before marriage, chose to be house-holders after marriage, just like my friend's mom and grandmother.

I expose my jealousy of my friend's delicious lunches to demonstrate the subtle passing on of family culture. I don't know the specifics of the women's choice of jobs, but cultural habits are not easy to overcome. My mom struggled with guilt, having to work instead of being at home raising children, like her mom. In another sense of culture, my wife of 15 years and I have achieved a measure of success in balancing family and cultural differences.

She's Polish, with dual Polish and US citizenship. Consistent with her native upbringing, she is concerned about rules and what neighbors think. I don't like rules and don't particularly care about what neighbors think, as long as I am pleasant and respect their rights. Adjusting to culture, though, whether of family or geography, can challenge the patience of a mime.

People in love, ravaged by pheromones and adoring opposites, are not concerned about diversity and the subtleties of family culture. But knowledge of the combustible nature of these passed-on-values might prove a useful tool with a relationship decision that could seesaw either way. Without understanding the power of culture, you might struggle throughout a relationship combating an unknown adversary.

Our Male or Female Nature

As we have seen, each gender has vastly different proportions of hormones and other mind-changing chemicals in their bodies, and are wired with different sex chromosomes in every one of their 40 trillion cells - XX if a girl and XY for boys. Her second X is six times the size his Y. **6 times!** In each extra "X" she has over 20 times the number of genes with their own instructions. If that isn't the most fundamental difference between sexes, then what is? Whether it's hunting, risk-taking, emotion, communication, competitiveness or any of the other takeaways discussed earlier, each gender's brains have to be directing them differently. **As I said previously, if she had his chromosomes and hormones she would act like him, and vice versa.**

How about brain functions given such instructions and hormones? Let's listen to what Dr. Gregory L. Jantz, internationally recognized author of over 26 books, generally about boys, has to say in his book ***Raising Boys by Design***. Dr. Jantz discusses how brain science influences raising and educating boys. He writes that boys' and girls' brains differ in four ways: processing, chemistry, structure, and blood flow. In a nutshell, this is what he explains about these four brain differences:

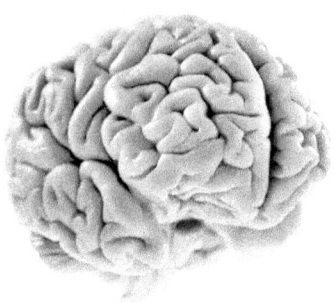

Your Standard Brain

• **Processing.** The brain of a man is comprised of nearly 7 times more *gray* matter than that of a female, while female brains utilize nearly 10 times more *white* matter. Gray matter is related to information and action-processing centers… White matter is the networking grid that connects the brain's gray matter with other processing centers. **Result:** The differences between gray and white matter explain why in adulthood **females are multi-taskers and men excel in highly task-focused projects.**

• **Chemistry**. Male and female brains process the same neurochemicals (i.e. serotonin - helps us sit still), testosterone (sex and aggression), estrogen (female growth and reproduction), and oxytocin (bonding and relationship), but to different degrees and through gender-specific connections. Males are not inclined to sit still as long as females and are more physically impulsive and aggressive. They process less oxytocin than females **(explains their reluctance to commit)**. **Result**: Boys need different strategies for stress release than girls, and are less likely to commit to a relationship.

• **Structure.** Females have a larger hippocampus, the human memory center in the brain, and a higher density of neural connections into the hippocampus. **Result:** Females absorb more sensorial and emotive information than males... Females have verbal centers on both sides of the brain, while males have verbal centers only on the left hemisphere. **Result:** Girls use more words telling stories or describing incidents, persons, objects, feelings or places. Males have fewer verbal centers and less connectivity between their word centers and their memories or feelings. **Thus**, girls have more interest in discussing feelings, emotions and senses.

• **Blood Flow and Brain Activity.** The female brain has a far more natural blood flow throughout the brain... and a higher degree of blood flow in a concentrated part of the brain called cingulate gyrus, which is related to ruminating on and revisiting emotional memories. Males tend, after reflecting more briefly on an emotional memory, to analyze and move to the next task (stay calm, taking it all in. *"Everything will be okay"*). They may also choose to change course and do something active and unrelated to feelings, rather than to analyze them. **Result: Blood flow explains how and why men and women argue so differently when provoked.**

Dr. Jantz goes on to point out that understanding gender differences from a neurological perspective not only opens the door to greater appreciation of the genders, but it also calls into question how we, as parents, educate and support our children from a young age.

Takeaways from brain function:

- **Females multi-task; men excel in highly task-focused projects** - Gray and White Matter differences.
- **Males can't sit still as long as females,** are more **physically impulsive and aggressive,** are **reluctant to commit** to a relationship, and **need different strategies for stress release** than girls - Chemistry.
- **Girls and women use more words** telling stories or describing anything, and have more interest in discussing feelings, emotions and senses due to brain structure.
- **Men and women argue differently** when provoked because of Blood flow.
- **Understanding brain differences leads to greater appreciation of genders, and calls into question how parents educate and support children from a young age.**

Three generations of Swedes have tinkered with gender equality, one of the cornerstones of Swedish society. The aim is to ensure that everyone enjoys the same opportunities, rights and obligations in all areas of life. Starting in preschool, the premise is that gender behavior is more environmentally inspired than biological, and therefore, if you want equality use teaching methods that counteract traditional gender patterns and roles to change what boys and girls do early in their lives, like pushing boys towards the arts and encouraging girls to yell. Personally, I like the way Swedes revolutionized dating. When I was young, guys had to pay on dates regardless of whether her family was rich or not. Guys also took the risks inherent in asking for a date and venturing towards the first kiss. But in Sweden, either gender could make the first move, and when they went out for dinner they split the bill. It's about equality. For parity now, American women would have to assume more risk to achieve physical intimacy, and more expense, which seems reasonable given women's increasing wage levels.

Although I like the concept of sharing risks and rewards, I believe equality between the sexes is a complex subject. After 2 million years of evolution, how do you equalize biology? And is emphasis on environmentally inspired behavior regarding equality good or bad? We have seen how the genders have different strengths. Females naturally dominate communication, and men are more competitive biologically. If teaching methods in school favor females, and male qualities, like aggression, are negatively considered except in thriller movies, wouldn't males continue to fall behind their female counterparts as our species continues to evolve? Today, girls have better grades in Swedish schools than boys and nearly 2/3 of all university degrees in Sweden are awarded to women. Is that equal? If we take the Swedish approach to achieve equality in education, would we miss out on the best each sex has to offer? That's my worry. I like what masculine and feminine convey in the pure sense of the words.

Appreciate and support him.
Have his back and pat it once in a while.

Our Unique Personality

Everyone is the center of their universe, with their own sense of truth and justice, perhaps because every human being has his or her unique genome, or set of genes. We are all wired differently, with different facts and ideas available to assess reality. Did you know there are three to four million differences between your genome and your neighbor's or your parents' genome?

When I was young I thought that everybody thought like me. But after years of marriage, business, travel, the single life and politics, it became clear to me that everyone has their own unique thought processes. I remember a friend saying when the U.S. was occupying Iraq, "I don't understand why they don't welcome us. We liberated them!" She couldn't sympathize with the feelings of a people being invaded by a foreign power. We think certain ideas are obvious, but not only do different people disagree on them—we are not always consistent ourselves. **We simply are what we inherit and what we experience.** Thought processes are like hair. We may have long hair, shaved hair, straight hair, curled hair or no hair. Republicans think differently from how Democrats think. Americans think differently from how Russians think. My thoughts are different from my wife's.

I thought I knew right and wrong. Then I traveled to foreign places and experienced completely different points of view. Points of view are like differences—the more you perceive, the more you understand. That's why Montaigne said of traveling, *"No propositions astonish me, no belief offends me, however much opposed to my own."*

At any given moment, our own unique personality can be split. Are you the same person with all your friends? Or, like me, are you different with different people? Serious with some, jovial with others; charming with some, grumpy with others; confident with some, unsure with others. Do you have multiple personalities?

Having grown up on the leading edge of technology in Silicon Valley and knowing how computers are constructed, I assumed I was the sum of my ancestors' knowledge and talents plus my own—heredity plus environment. I knew we had ample memory in our bodies to store vast knowledge accumulated through the ages. That was my point of view before a bus ride.

PART 1 DIFFERENCES   *5. Differences That Define Us – Specific*

Story: *Travelling on a bus to visit Osho's ashram in Poona, India, I sat next to an old man with a long, white beard and matching white robe. During the bumpy ride across dusty ditches in the road, as the bus dodged oblivious sacred cows and ubiquitous people, some in colorful flowing dresses and others in gray tatters, we talked. I told him I couldn't rationalize reincarnation.*

"Why?" he asked.

"Because I believe we are the sum of what our ancestors passed on to us plus what we experience. How can we be this biological spirit and also be a reincarnated spirit?"

He said simply, "Why can we not be both?"

That answer bugged me for miles and miles. Then a light turned on. Why not? Why can't we have one spirit based on biology and other spirits who choose to inhabit us for some reason? The old man said little, but what he said was big. Multiple spirits come equipped with a smorgasbord of talents and personalities that we can use to accomplish a mission, or vision, for instance.

So, I ask you, "Are you a woman who wants to make men happy?" If so, call upon that spirit within you that can make a man happy. If we are controlled by our subconscious 90% of the time, let's delegate: use your conscious 10% to put the subconscious 90% to work in order to accomplish this lofty goal.

Time Frames We Live In: Past, Present, Future, All Three.

The theory I find most provocative is this: most people live predominantly in one time frame—past, present or future—and they pop in and out of the others.

"He seems to be stuck in the past.
"Live in the present. Smell the flowers."
"She's always dreaming of the future."

The Present (in the moment)

In the moment is good sex, the thrill of your first base hit, basket or goal, your first kiss, the day you fell in love, movies and popcorn, connecting with someone and feeling textures and emotions around you. In the moment, you have time to notice people and see their facial expressions, time to empathize and time to laugh. Humor is in the moment.

Story: In a place called Pokhara, in Nepal, I was rowing a boat with a friend. As we drifted on placid Lake Pewa, surrounded by the bright green early rice under the shadow of snowy Mount Everest, we were content to absorb a quiet so loud you could hear a minnow splash. In this quiet, we discussed living in the present. She had recently come from Papaji's ashram.

"Feel the energy," she urged softly. "Papaji says freedom is living in the now."

She picked up a paddle as I slouched comfortably. "Freedom is also watching someone else paddle," I replied.

Smiling briefly at the comment, she continued. "Papaji teaches that we are pure consciousness in the absolute here and now—

already and always free! You don't need to attain it. You just need to realize it. He says by quieting the mind we remove the world of thoughts and desires that the mind believes are real. Papaji says when your identification with the unreal has vanished, you will be what you have been, the spirit.

*"When I told my friends about your trip around the world, they asked your age. Then they said, 'A midlife crisis trip!' They can't conceive of wanting freedom for its own sake, as opposed to rebellion … Happiness is now. People always plan for their happiness tomorrow, but often don't know what makes them happy today." (**The Traveler** by yours truly)*

I lived this freedom for several years. I had no responsibility at the time. My kids had graduated from college; my former wife was finishing her PhD thesis in psychology; and I had earned enough money to buy security while I was traveling. Living in the present means less time thinking about the past or future. The past might be painful; the future, unknown, and the unknown might be fearful.

Some people, good managers for instance, have the ability to balance all three time frames, past, present and future. You may ask, "What difference does it make which time frame you live in?" **A lot!** The downside to predominately living in the present, for instance, is that money concerns often make life difficult. Also, most conflict between people is part of a dynamic with tentacles into the past that are not articulated in the present. Who does what around the house, for instance. When those tentacles are triggered, consequences wiggle into the now.

Sweet Sue said, "When I have an argument with him, he never seems to remember the past, **so we do the same things over and over that don't work.** I want to change the dynamic, but he won't admit its existence."

A mother who lives predominantly in the present constantly micro-manages her husband on how to prepare their child's breakfast. To the first five reminders he may not respond, and then the repetition gets on his nerves. She doesn't remember the reminders because they are in the past. So when he eventually reacts negatively towards her, she is offended.

Result: A small misunderstood or forgotten dynamic triggers a huge argument.

Anger often originates from past transgressions triggered by present activities. Those who focus on the now and have a vague memory of the past seem confused by this type of anger. Wisdom, however, is putting two and two together. Spanish essayist, George Santayana, says, *"Those who cannot remember the past are condemned to repeat it!"*

The Past

A star in high school or college loves the past. As **Coach** said in the movie **Hoosiers,** "Most people never get to experience being a star. What's wrong with that?" Everything is fine unless you decide not to move on. The character played by Dennis Hopper in the same movie, missed being a star by a half inch. He considered himself a loser, consigned to the devil, drowning in alcohol. Sometimes the past houses our greatest achievements and memories, like our first kiss, the day we graduated, or falling in love. Let's face it, everything that has happened up to now is in our memory, in the past. I like to reminisce about the past. Sure, there were troubles. But many of the great events in your life happened in the past. Why not relive them? It took me eight years to write my two travel adventures and memoirs, **Breaking Free** and **The Traveler.** That's eight years living much of my time in the past. Those were wonderful years.

Unfortunately, like Dennis Hopper's character, some people can't move out of the past. They are unable to smell the flowers' fragrance, because of a perceived failure they are desperately compelled to reiterate, to ruminate over as if they could change something. People with positive attitudes, however, move on.

Trouble's not that hard to get out of, unless you've killed somebody or have already been sentenced. I spent 10 years in Silicon Valley building companies and an equal number of years fixing them. To fix a troubled business you need to quickly understand the past, and cope with the present while developing a plan to fix problems and create opportunity in the future. Fixing or creating is a multi time-frame endeavor.

Story: *One day my wife got a phone call from my daughter's best friend. She was babysitting in Santa Cruz for "a sweet thirties-something couple with two adorable kids." She said they were having money trouble and wanted to talk to me. My wife said, "Denis doesn't handle individuals, but just in case he agrees to talk, prepare a list of monthly income and expenses on separate sheets of paper." She added they should develop one goal for the future.*

I hadn't been to Santa Cruz for a while, and I thought the fresh-air drive along the Pacific would be therapeutic.

I knocked on the door, walked into the couple's house and met Stary, a cute, thin, plain-looking woman, about 5'6". "Is your husband home?" I asked, "I'd like to talk to both of you." The place had three bedrooms and the 70-year-old wooden architecture was befitting to your average 30s-something couple. Through the open back door I saw a swing in the yard, a playhouse, trodden grass and a big tree with low hanging branches that one of the truly adorable children was hanging on.

Stary handed me two sheets of paper. "He asked if you could meet him at the new house," she said.

I looked down briefly at the sheets. The first page, labeled "Income," had one line item. The second sheet, "Expenses," was filled from top to bottom with line items. "New house?" I said. "How do I get there?"

"Our strategy," she blurted out, "is for me to finish the children's book I'm writing. It will be a bestseller and we can get ourselves out of debt. There are expenses on the list that I can't avoid if I want to reach that vision." She was lobbying. "My husband, Jacob, is a game programmer for a Silicon Valley company." The one item on the "Income" list had been recorded as $90,000. "But I think you can cut a lot of Jacob's expenses on the list. He tends to be a good old Joe with his friends." She struck me as naive, positive and a peach of a person.

I went over to the new house, a block from the ocean. The yard was made for barbecues—all concrete. Jacob, tall, gaunt and as sad-looking as his drooping mustache, said he had put his $35,000 bonus from a video game he developed into buying this house. That's what friends had advised him to do. In answer to my next question, he said the other house was a rental and they were moving into this new one, whose mortgage payments were $5,000 a month. I mentioned $5,000 was the amount their monthly expenses exceeded their monthly income. He said that sounded right because $5,000 was the amount they put on each new credit card. He said they had about 25 cards and were adept at finagling interest and principal. He added that he hated the new house. Then he asked if we could walk along the beach and talk.

I wasn't in a hurry, and walking on a California beach is heaven. Walking barefoot in shorts, he confided openly that his financial troubles weighed so heavily on him that lately he'd been thinking seriously of abandoning his family and running away somewhere. He said his sleepless nights were filled with guilt over his present thoughts and past spending. He said he felt trapped.

I told him he could stop thinking of running away. His problems were manageable. He could sell the new house, which was an albatross around his neck, and scale back the spending to create a cushion for a rainy day. The new house had no place for the kids to play anyway.

"But we might lose money if we sell."

"You might, but you will be able to live your life under financial control without guilt. What's that worth to you?"

We returned to the rental house. Stary had spread papers on their dining room table. She had defined one goal for their future: to live within their means. We reviewed the "Expenses" list of line items. They all seemed to be $300 a month.

"Do you guys get sick a lot?" I asked, startled by the first item.

"Why?"

"Because $300 a month seems like a lot for drugs."

"Oh!" She laughed. *"That's for marijuana. But Jacob said he's going to quit, so cross it off the list."* She was so sure of herself.

Then we talked about her book. *"I don't want to be discouraging or callous,"* I said, *"but the odds of you winning the lottery are probably better than writing a bestseller. Even if you were to win, it would take time. Fixing finances is a pragmatic affair. It's not desire that counts, so much as habit. You need to habitually live within your means."* We went back and forth on expenses. She was alive with ideas, and he went along with them.

Stary said, *"My mother said she would pay for art supplies, so cross off those three line items."*

"My friends and I are inventors," Jacob said. *"We need to read a lot of magazines for ideas. But cross magazines out,"* he ordered with a sweep of the arm, as if channeling his wife's enthusiasm through osmosis. *"I'm always buying the technical mags. Let them pay!"*

We agreed on this bottom-line: they would sell the house, cut spending as planned and thus save $2,000 a month. So far so good. I suggested, *"Take the $3,500 monthly spending budget we agreed on and write four checks for $875 each. Cash one check each week to fund expenses."*

The blood drained from their faces. It turned out that they had never written a check and were frightened by the thought of it! They handled money through credit cards, which intrigued me. So, the final deal was that they would keep a stock of dried beans. Every week *they would put 175 beans in a cookie jar, each bean representing $5. The beans totaled $875, the amount of their weekly budget. During the week, they would add up credit charges or cash spent and remove the corresponding number of beans from the jar. When they ran out of their weekly ration of beans, they would eat soup.*

Result: *Jacob used Stary's optimism regarding the future to pull himself out of his present desperation. Hope was alive!*

With everyone satisfied, I drove north along the Pacific Ocean towards home. As if a reward for doing the good deed, I experienced a once-in-a-lifetime thrill. A sea-lion, the size of a pickup truck, had beached itself, having been bitten on its bottom flank by a giant white shark (I presumed). It lay there, struggling to survive. With just the two of us on that windy beach, I was careful of its mammoth front teeth as I attempted to soothe the beast. When crowds and phones arrived, I left.

The Future

Living predominantly in the future has its karma. The future holds promise and solutions. Hunters migrated to fertile new lands chock-full of caribou. Entrepreneurs visualize their dream using a plan, and then they search for money-lenders and investors to finance their vision. Their plan being the roadmap to that future.

Story: *I have always had an eye on the future, probably because my vision of it played such a significant role in my life. Learning how to use the powers of prediction and achievement put me in an ideal position for growing and fixing companies, raising the family I wanted, and later leaving business to pursue prolonged travel.*

PART 1 DIFFERENCES   5. Differences That Define Us – Specific

As a senior at Providence College I sent expensive applications to graduate schools to obtain an MBA and shield myself from the insanity of the Vietnam War. Because I was a C+ student with a love for basketball, I couldn't get a job interview with my roommate, much less companies recruiting students on campus, and I received "thanks but no thanks" letters from at least 15 graduate schools. The last response I received was from Denver University offering me, to my delirious surprise, a full scholarship. Later, after a long, expansive drive to the university, I went to the administrative office to meet the dean of Business School Admissions and ask why in the world they had given me a scholarship?

A thin pensive man looked up my file, which was stashed in a steel filing cabinet next to his desk. After reviewing the contents of a manila folder, he looked at me curiously and said, "Well, it wasn't your grades! But I did note you consistently aced your major ... Every year we pick one student who otherwise would not be qualified for our program, but who we feel would be a credit to this institution in the future. This year, you're that person."

"Why?" I asked, puzzled.

He leaned back in his reclining chair for a moment, as if assessing me. "It was your letter about who you would be in the future that caught our attention. You expressed a passion for and description of a future that persuaded us to take the chance."

In all my years fixing troubled companies, I never saw one that had a good plan for the future. What does that reveal? Those who achieve more out of life visualize and think clearly about their future. Some people are forced to, like those in cold-weather countries who plan for winter as a matter of survival. Eventually they developed planning skills that, over time, earned them a much higher standard of living than those in warm countries, where you pick food off trees and build a new school when the old one falls down. Vision leads to growth, culturally or personally. But first you need to clear cobwebs.

Yuval Harari said that being allowed to admit our ignorance after 1500 AD led to spectacular growth over the next 500 years, because a natural reaction to admitting you are wrong is to find out why. For 1500 years, religion stymied growth by persecuting those whose thoughts might prove religious dogma (cobweb) wrong; for example, the earth is the center of the universe. I feel compassion for the great artists of those times. They must have been chomping at the bit to paint something more stimulating than legions of chubby angels and devious devils armed with bows and arrows and spears. Those creatures were the only game in town for that long dark age. Painters like Salvador Dali or the Impressionists had no such limitations.

The future we want may fall short, but look at what happened to Stary and Jacob in Santa Cruz when they created a plan for the future. To finish that story, ten years later, at my around-the-world going-away party, they told me they were smelling flowers and living without fear of debt. They had eaten lots of soup in the past 10 years, they said, and were still counting their beans.

Differences define who we are. We are born into our family culture, born with a male or female nature, born with our unique personality, and probably born with the time frame we live in. Understanding these differences is like speaking Polish. If you want to understand Polish people, you need to speak their language.

6. Do Women "Get" Men?

Old cliché: Women marry men to change them. Men marry women hoping they won't change.

Dr. Brizendine says in ***The Man's Brain,*** "Women have a deep misunderstanding of the biological and social instincts that drive men. As women, we love men, live with men and their son, but we have yet to understand men and boys." Let's do a quick check. Below are a few common statements by men. Are any of them relevant to you?

- "I am NOT a mind-reader. If you want something from me, say it. Hints don't work."
- "It's Sunday sports time. Either watch with me or let me be. Please!"
- "Come to me with a problem only if you want help solving it. That's what we do!"
- "Either ask me to do something or tell me how you want it done. Not both. If you know the best way to do it, tell me up front."
- "If you ask a question that you don't want an answer to, expect an answer you don't want to hear."

Would you say "gatherers" are prone to receiving these comments from hunters because of how both sexes communicate?

Story: On a beach on the Cambodian coast along the Gulf of Thailand, young touts roamed the blond sands selling broiled lobster tail, roasted calamari and scrumptious thick potato chips. My friend, Andy, was in a deep discussion about prostitutes with a woman from Amsterdam, whose husband lounged and listened on the beach chair behind her, out of her line of sight. They were discussing what was obvious to a man traveling alone or with other men in Cambodia, but not so obvious to a woman. Andy was saying that from a male traveler's point of view, prostitutes were ubiquitous in Cambodia. Then the conversation took a twist.

"No man I know would go to a prostitute!" the rather prim, long-haired 30-year-old insisted. Her generously tanned husband winced visibly behind her, while she cleared a lock of hair from her forehead.

"How many men have you asked?" Andy pursued.

"What?"

He rephrased. "Have you asked any man you know if he's been with a prostitute?"

I glanced at her husband. He shrugged at me with a look that said, "She didn't ask me!"

"Well, no," she replied after a dab of thought. "But I know they wouldn't. None of them is that kind of man."

The husband flashed a sheepish grin.

"Why would a perfectly healthy man ever go to one?" she continued, looking to the ocean as if it held the answer.

Several moments of silence passed, during which I watched the waves roll in to shore, pause for a moment and then retreat.

"Because it's fun," Andy answered. "Most men I know have been with a prostitute at some point in their life. They would consider a nocturnal visit a rite of passage, I suppose … although they may not tell anyone, especially a woman."

I thought of my brother, who could have no opportunity with women unless he paid a prostitute. His mind worked slower than others did. He was dumpy and didn't have the confidence to approach a woman for a date. Should he go without for a lifetime?

Oblivious to her husband's body language, she concluded, "It doesn't seem right."

George Carlin's point of view was this: "I don't understand why prostitution is illegal. Selling is legal. Fucking is legal. Why isn't selling fucking legal? Why should it be illegal to sell something that is perfectly legal to give away. Of all the things you can do, giving someone an orgasm is hardly the worst thing in the world."

I came away from the beach discussion wondering how much she understood men. She could have grabbed the opportunity to get into their head if she had been open. Did she think the men she knew thought the way she thought? Would her sex life improve if she spent more time finding out how guys are put together? Understanding men's view of sex cuts through a ton of hypocrisy.

What do you think?

Much has been postulated about how men and women separate love and sex—that women combine love and sex more than men do. I've always felt that men are starved of intimacy. The women I've known always seen to have a female best friend for intimacy, and they discuss their sex life with that person. Most men I've known avoid discussing the intimate details of another guy's wife, girlfriend or lover. It's sort of considered taboo among men. Sex allows men a measure of intimacy that seems hard to distinguish from love sometimes. I believe men crave intimacy, and sex feels like it much of the time.

Hint. On a conservative note, if you desire a solid relationship with a man from the beginning, you might want to add logs to his flame, but hold sex back until you have explored him. Maybe it's the cave mentality, but I believe most men would wonder about faithfulness if you jumped into the sack first thing. Plus, waiting increases intimacy, don't you think?

Changing men. **Women marry men to change them.** While there are benefits to changing a man, there are also pitfalls:
- In the extreme, eventually you become a nag.
- You lose touch with *him.* You try to change him into *you,* thus losing the man you fell in love with. Isn't that what changing him means? Creating someone else! Who's better than you?

Changing men is Sisyphus struggling to push that monstrous rock up and up and up. People change when they want to change or have incentive.

Hint: There are ways to get him to do things. Incentivize!

Story: After two years working together, my business partner and I had a few major issues between us that could damage our partnership—like being late for meetings! We decided to pick two issues apiece that we wanted the other to change. The deal: Whoever didn't resolve each issue within three months to the satisfaction of the other would shell out $1,500 each. **The result:** Not a dime creased the other's hand. Money was a great motivator for both of us.

My father had addictions. First alcohol. When he quit drinking, he glommed onto Miracle Whip for the sugar hit. He put Miracle Whip on everything—coffee, eggs, even steak. My brother, never on the *best terms with Dad, bet him $50 he couldn't abstain from Miracle Whip for six months. The money may not seem like a lot for some people, but for my father it was an incentive. Six months later, Mom called my brother. "You know, dear," she said, "your father says you owe him $50."*

"Huh?"

"You did make a bet with him on Miracle Whip," she said, ever so sweetly.

Silence! "You mean he hasn't eaten Miracle Whip for six months?"

"That's right, dear!"

"The money is on the way. Jesus, Mom, do you know what this means? We can take a collection from family members and for $300 dollars a year we can get rid of all his bad habits. We'll probably be over-subscribed."

Point: Negotiate with your man—or make a bet! What does he want in return? List three negotiating assets you have. Suggestion: Sex, food, football. Keep the fulfillment period short and renew the wager at regular intervals, if necessary, to cement change. Men marry women hoping they don't change. That's opportunity knocking at your door! Even rocks change, but you can negotiate a little change for something you want from him. For example, you want him to shave and look nice in the morning? Negotiate! You want him to go dancing with you? Negotiate! What does he get in return? Men fall for a dream, right? Dreams are in our head, but they need nourishment to survive. So ... nourish!

A few negotiating tactics.

- Separate the person from the issue. Put yourself in his shoes (reread chapters 1–3). Listen to and acknowledge what he is saying, and give him a stake (or steak) in the outcome.

Rather than defending your ideas, invite advice. Remember, admitting mistakes leads to growth.
- Focus on interests, not positions. Ask why and why not. The most important issues are basic human needs.
- Summarize what you both agreed to.

Advice: The most important thing in negotiating or making bets is that you must pay up. Otherwise, you lose trust!

Simplify with a Honey-do list (with emphasis on honey). Lists are a measure of independence for a guy. Males like to do things at their own pace, without anyone bugging them. It's a hunter thing. The essence of their self-esteem is a measure of independence. Lists work! Unless you have a dud, he gets the job done faster. Lists avoid arguments.

Simplify using 80-20 rule. I'll bet the average guy, even above-average, will seldom perform better than 80% on any chore he's given to do around the house. That would pertain to most jobs you want him to do. What typically happens, and I've seen this over and over, including with myself, is that she requires 100%. He quickly realizes he can't satisfy her and gives up. Chances are you've discouraged him for future jobs of this nature. One thing I learned in business is that 80% is a lot better than nothing. If, in the long term, you need 100% from him, you should get another partner. But my suspicion is you will always be disappointed and overworked.

Encourage. Criticism eats away trust and respect.

Victim/bad-guy script

From a guy's point of view, the #1 issue with his woman is what I call "victim/bad-guy script or syndrome." This script has guilt subliminally written throughout. Guilt that eats at men from the heart to the brain. Free him from bad-guy guilt and he'll be a happy man. In all likelihood, genetic programing and millions of

DNA instructions have hardwired our roles, to the extent I doubt most women even know this syndrome exists.

But let's find out. Has the man in your life complained about being the "bad guy"? If so, have his bad-guy complaints given you pause to think? Every man I've ever talked to, in or out of a relationship, hates being **bad-guy.** It's my biggest issue, and just recently my friend, Colin, said, "There have been times in my relationships with women that I have been no-jury-would-ever-convict-me, without-the-slightest-doubt innocent. But because of an inadvertent slip, a word used in frustration, I wound up guilty. I hate that!"

Here's how bad-guy script plays out in the movie **Tortilla Soup.**

Story: *Tortilla Soup is about a Cuban family. The characters include the father, who owns a busy gourmet Mexican restaurant and catering service, and his three daughters, age 29, 27 and 18. They adore their dad but are struggling with moving out of his house. The older daughter finds a boyfriend after many years, marries and moves out. The middle daughter, holding an MBA, grapples with relocating to Spain to pursue an entrepreneurial endeavor. It's highly likely she will indeed go to Spain. The younger daughter wants to be grown up in her family's eyes, so, unbeknownst to everyone, she makes her own decision not to go to college. When her dad finds out, she argues with him in front of her boyfriend, who just watches in silence. During the argument, she spontaneously announces that she is moving out of the house and in with the very surprised boyfriend. In the following month, this daughter rearranges her boyfriend's home and makes it neat and clean, just the way she likes. She notices neither his reticence nor his reaction to missing papers, including what* *is later revealed to be his letter of acceptance to the same college she would have attended had she not acted so rashly.*

He finally becomes irritated with her and points out, rather meekly, that she hadn't consulted him before the initial move-in or for any subsequent adjustments she made to his apartment. She gets upset, throws a tantrum and tosses his now neatly arranged papers all over the floor. She cries, declares how much she's improved the place and rebukes him for his lack of appreciation. He's the bad guy—guilty and forlorn. He apologizes for his actions.

What causes this syndrome? Perhaps Dr. Brizendine can enlighten us. In **The Female Brain,** she states, "the teen girl's brain makes her feel powerful, always right, and blind to consequences. Without that drive, she'll never be able to grow up … Her girl power includes premenstrual syndrome, sexual competition, and controlling girl groups …" She further explains in **The Male Brain** that "the female brain tends to run negative scenarios to protect itself from disappointment and then place the blame on the male brain, like pinning the tail on the donkey … When a man's partner is critical of him, his brain goes on the defensive."

She concludes, "if I can impart one lesson to women that I learned in writing these books, it would be that understanding biology of the male brain helps us relate better to the male reality … Much of the conflict that exists between men and women is fueled by unrealistic expectations that stem from failing to grasp each other's innate differences."

Am I overstating the syndrome? Check it out. Be empirical. Be empathetic. Ask around. Then, if you agree that this victim/bad-guy syndrome exists, here is what you can do when the situation requires: listen to him using Maslow's listening definition below.

Adam Maslow's definition of listening:

"... listen ..., wholly passively, self-effacingly listen -- without presupposing, classifying, improving, controverting, evaluating, approving or disapproving, without dueling with what is being said, without rehearsing the rebuttal in advance, without free-associating to portions of what is being said so that succeeding portions are not heard at all ..."

What Works for Guys

- **Accept what you cannot change, negotiate what you can.**
- **Simplify:** give him a honey-do list and abide by the 80/20 rule.
- **Make him a good guy.**
- **Listen, using Maslow's definition.**

Summary of Chapters 1-6

- **Do 1 thing for your hunter - your dad, boyfriend, grandfather, uncle, brother or friend.**
- **Understand differences between you and him. Remember to ask questions, because love is an exploration.**
- **Appreciate and support him. Have his back and pat it once in a while.**
- **Accept what you cannot change, negotiate what you can.**
- **Simplify: give him a honey-do list and abide by the 80/20 rule.**
- **Make him a good guy.**
- **Listen, using Maslow's definition.**

PART 2
HAPPY GUYS

7. Raw Sex, Please

"Nineteen ways to light his fire! You know what it takes to light his fire?"
"What?"
"You show up!"
(Six Days Seven Nights)

"With such a horny force animating every microscopic detail of ourselves, we should think of all human needs as sub-needs arising from the desire to procreate. Our hunger for love, our ambitions, our desire to belong, our urge to make beautiful things, our need to talk, our voracious curiosity, our fear of death, our longing for transcendence, our willingness to die for our community, our ache for God. All our qualities evolved to the extent they serve the reproduction of genes in ourselves and our beloved annoying relatives."— Joe Quirk

HOW TO MAKE A MAN HAPPY

Story: She said with a touch of slut in her hungry eyes, "Come over at 6 o'clock for dinner ... and fun." The excitement lacing her voice caused his blood to stir. At six sharp, he knocked on her door, smelling fresh and sexy and dressed neat and tight, top buttons open exposing brown curly hair. She was dressed to kill: raven dark hair swirling down her shoulders, ruby red lipstick, tight jeans and sexy blouse showcasing her delicious décolletage. She greeted him with a soft fleshy kiss that said, "Sooo glad you're here!"

The cozy kitchen table was adorned with a white lace tablecloth, two place settings and two full glasses of aged Merlot. She led him to his seat, waltzed to the stove and prepared their meal. She glanced his way occasionally, sporting a seductive smile. "Comfortable?" she asked.

His mouth watered as blood circulated in a steam of anticipation.

Every five minutes or so she sauntered over, sat on his lap and kissed him strong, her tongue penetrating, searching ... communicating ... demanding! He matched her intensity, transformed into an explorer. Then she stood and calmly walked back to resume cooking. During dinner she teased him, her eyes flirting ... inviting him to taste what she had not yet divulged. She was in total control!

After dinner, modest discussion and immodest touch, she rose from the table, picked up a kitchen chair, carried it into the hallway and placed it facing the bathroom entrance.

"What is she doing?" He wondered.

She went to the living room, to an oak table with glass inlay and a slot for a CD player, near her comfortable couch. She picked up the remote, turned on Ravel's Bolero and eyed him on her way back to the kitchen. Tossing a naughty smile his way, she grabbed his hand, led him to the hallway chair and motioned for him to sit. Before she *could escape, though, he pulled her in for a wild kiss. Released, she rubbed against his shoulder, stood up and started to move away, her right hand dropping back and sliding almost to his crotch, and then sauntered into the bathroom. With that touch, the pressure down under sparked a stampede of millions of anxious sperm—a delirious sensation.*

She turned the shower spigot on, checked the temperature and faced him as he sat bewitched. Wetting her lips with her tongue and narrowing her eyes, she strolled back to the doorway in front of his chair and began to unbutton her blouse.

"Help me," she asked.

He smiled, and rose for the occasion. "Absolutely!"

Piece by piece by piece, he undressed her until her body was bare. His blood boiled. Then, her long hair shining, she walked into the shower and turned to face him again. Her smile paralyzed him. She bathed while he gazed, lovestruck and extended. After washing off the suds, she stepped from the shower, put on a bathrobe and grabbed his hand, directing him towards the music and the couch.

Bolero's relentless rhythm now pulsated to the point where its demanding beat drew closer and closer to climax.

The evening started anew.

Ladies, you can easily pull off this guy's dream for your man. Initiate! Excitement, mystery, fantasy. Pheromones or no pheromones, women control sex. We hunters become like dogs following a steak bone. When we get excited about you, it ignites a nuclear reaction that howls for release. Control the manhood and you control the man! Use that "bad girl" button embedded in the extra X to plan a night he'll remember.

Is sex really that important?

Story: At work one day, sitting at my desk pondering, I asked a very talented associate, who'd stopped in for a quick chat, what percentage of the day he thinks about women. Mitch responded with raised eyebrow and a quick reply. "Not that much."

Three hours later, he poked his head into my office and said matter-of-factly, "I guess I think about women around 15% of my day."

"Including sleeping hours?"

"Yeah."

Making the calculation mentally, I said, "That's three and a half hours. If you deduct a day's work of, say, 11 hours plus time for sleep from 24 hours, your three and a half hours are in fact... almost 30% of your remaining available time. That's a lot."

"That would be about right. But you'd probably have to modify that, because sometimes I think about women during the day ... when work allows it."

I was shocked by his admission. I got up and closed the door. "When does work allow it? What kind of sex?"

"You mean, what do I think about?"

"Yeah!"

"Why?"

"Because I'm curious to see if you're like me."

Ask Mitch an honest question and he'll give an honest answer. "Well, if you really want to know, I can't avoid looking at women walking. They're art! I fantasize about fucking or going down on my wife's best friend. Or undressing in my mind half the female population. Most times I can't help what comes into my mind when it comes to sex. Does that answer your question?"

"Yeah. Let's get back to work."

Be anthropologically kinky, ladies. Just the thought of it makes me feel deviant myself—warped, perverted. It's in our genes. Sex with more than one person, fantasy or S&M à la 50 Shades of Grey. Over 125 million copies of the book were sold worldwide by 2015. To mostly women. Like it or not, kinky is fun, thrilling and an anthropological phenomenon, probably dating back to our cave-dwelling days. Practice! Practice! Practice! Get kinky. Let your hair go wild. Spanking, domination—whatever strikes your fancy. Who cares what the neighbors think? So what if you're in your 50s, 60s or 80s? So what if you're shy? It's normal! Your ancestors passed this particular wrinkle forward.

Hint: Encourage your guy to come hither. Otherwise he may think you're not interested and stop initiating sex. Sexual risk-taking may not come easy to most men.

Warning: Do not send naked pictures via email or the internet! Email and the internet have no security. Your photos could end up anywhere.

Date nights

are special. He gets intimacy and, if he plays his cards right, sex. Dress down and sexy. Tell him he turns you on. He's your hero. Guys get off on being your hero. Don't forget those sweeter-than-wine DNA kisses! Check out this dialogue:

Her: "What do you think of my dress?"
Him: "I want to take it off."
Her: "You mean you don't like it?"
Him: "No, I love it! That's why I want to take it off."

iPhones.

Sext him! Regale him with a sweet text message. "You are the man for me. My hero makes me …!" or "You make me so happy, babe!" or "I think of you all the time, my cumquat!" (or fruit of your choice). "The mere thought of you makes me hot!" Limit phone usage when you're with him, except to show pictures that provoke excitement. Guys like to be the center of your attention.

I conducted a small survey about whether it's acceptable to check the phone of someone close to you for possible cheating. The response was 50-50. Fifty percent felt someone checking their messages was an invasion of privacy. Fifty percent did not. If someone checked my messages I would lose trust in that person.

Porn and fantasy. My experience is that women enjoy porn but are often shy and hesitant to initiate watching it. So, he initiates. A time comes when the guy feels he's exhausted his opportunity and quits. What does she do? Remember in the Swedish model! She initiates fantasy too. That's sexual equality in risk-taking. The longer the relationship, the more you need spice to keep romance alive and sparkling. Porn is spice. Pure fantasy. If you are a storyteller, create fantasy for him. His rapture and yours should be priceless. Do you see the rapture in your mind's eye? Better yet, he adds a juicy scene.

Suggestion: Avoid moralizing about porn movies. They're porn movies! Also don't laugh.

Not Too Anxious.

Story: My wife and I had dinner with a friend who was closing in on 40. She was upset and angry. She had recently lost her boyfriend. During the meal we learned that she had known him for six weeks, had initially waited two weeks for him to call and hadn't seen him for the last two weeks. Quick math revealed a two-week hot-and-heavy affair. The man was 42 and had never been married.

When fishing for men, you need only a little bait. Cast the lure. Jiggle it. When you get a bite, don't rip the line from the water. Play hard-to-get and maneuver the prey home. A guy that hasn't been married at 42 is more likely to cut and run than to rush into a relationship. Lots of jiggling is needed to land this guy, and lots of letting him run with the lure. Dig into the deeper picture: Why is he single? Is he jinxed? Or is he extremely fussy? Even the playboy generally gets married at some point.

What is the thinking behind the woman's actions in this story?

Story: *A guy has a great evening of sex with his lover. They take a bath together, followed by a candlelit dinner during which they discuss all sorts of subjects including their lust for each other. They round out the evening having ecstatically wild sex. He'll want a repeat performance the next night. Guaranteed!*

"Let's do the same tomorrow," he says confidently.

"I would love to," she replies, satisfied.

The next night, he waits in bed, hope ringing eternal. She's in the bathroom getting ready. She comes out in flannel pajamas and gets into bed with zero fanfare and goes to sleep.

"How is that possible?" he wonders, feeling annoyed and discarded as his thing softens under the covers.

Random thoughts about guys: If you have difficulty telling him what feels good to you, advise him gingerly. If he takes your advice, he's a keeper. If you like to give abundant instruction, please yourself and have him watch. Remember, women have a good girl and a harlot inside. Guys like both.

- Avoid using sex as a weapon. It backfires!
- If you turn down his sexual invites consistently, he may stop having sex with you altogether. Hunter's ego.
- Sexual activity creates desire, and desire creates sexual activity.
- A female in orgasm spurs a man's satisfaction and fuels his dreams.
- Date men whose marriage is ending, or about to, at your peril. They need more sex then than any one person can possibly supply.

Discussing your sex life together.

Story: *Just the other night, my wife and I were discussing sex-education in Polish schools with friends. It was dinner conversation in Warsaw where we live. Our Polish friends, one a grade school teacher, told us sex education was difficult to implement because the words used, like penis and vagina, might be considered impolite and offensive in Polish circles. We talked about how, given senstivity to sex-related words, sex education was even possible.*

My eighth grade teacher, Sister Lucy, explained to our class that, "sex is for procreation in marriage, and if the couple enjoyed it, well that was a side benefit." Of course, the procreation or recreation priority has been reversed today, fortunately for recreation oriented people and the movie industry, which seems convinced that sex is a requisite early scene for a large proportion of movies.

Mulling over the conversation later that night, it occurred to me that the aversion to teaching sex education to school children might be related to people's discomfort in discussing their own sex lives with their partners. How many arguments could be avoided if we talked openly about our sexual needs, like what we like and don't like our partners to do, or changes to our libido as we age? How many couples talk to each other about sex or discuss sex education openly with their children?

With that out-of-the-way, let's discuss male sexual organs.

The penis is a muscle. He uses it or he loses it. "*It has to* be essentially exercised," says Tobias Kohler, MD, assistant professor of urology at the Southern Illinois University School of Medicine, in an article by Martin Downs, MPH, titled "Sensitivity, *Pleasure*, Size and Other Surprising Facts." He writes, *"To maintain a healthy tone, the smooth muscle of the penis must be periodically enriched with oxygen by the rush of blood that engorges the penis and makes it erect."*

The Pleasure Zone.

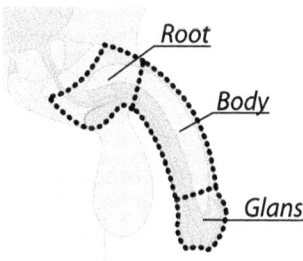

(British Journal of Urology International, 2009)

Researchers asked 81 healthy men to rate the erotic sensitivity of different areas of their bodies, the penis and zones such as the scrotum, anus, nipples and neck. The undersides of the glans and shaft (body) had the highest rating of sensitivity to sexual pleasure, followed by the upper side of the glans. Other researchers also report that as a man becomes more and more sexually aroused, the glans becomes less and less sensitive. If there are times when he can't climax during intercourse, they suggest stimulating with oral sex. **Also, that old bugaboo about men conking out after intercourse** rather than cuddling may be because his shot of oxytocin during sex acts like a sleeping pill afterwards.

Vibrators work on the penis too. Kohler says vibration is so effective on the penis that often men with spinal cord injuries can ejaculate with the aid of a special medical vibrator. The vibrator is usually held against the underside of the head of the penis. When patients see him about difficulty reaching orgasm, he suggests a store-bought personal vibrating massager.

What Works for Guys

**Don't forget the spice.
Dress to thrill and be anthropologically kinky.**

8. Low Hanging Fruit

Romance Cheat Sheet for lovers

The following are romance tips from my book, *How to Make a Woman Happy*, and other tips that apply to making a *man* happy. These are low hanging fruit which are easy to pick and fit into a busy day.

Be appreciative and loving. Send a card, email or text message containing a love poem or a simple statement that says you love and appreciate him. We all need a compliment and appreciation now and again.

Be adventurous. Make love in nature … or against the wall … slow or wild. How about a picnic? A fun night of laughing and dancing … an evening drive in the moonlight … wine and cheese. Hold him on the beach at sunset … or at an intimate small-town hideaway … on top of a mountain … or up on the roof.

Be bad. Engage in promiscuous love. Tell him you're wearing no underwear in public. Bring out the bad girl that resides within. After all, how often does a good woman take the opportunity to be bad? Be inspired by or replicate the scene at the start of chapter 7.

Be imaginative. Create a ritual, like pizza at Tony's on Friday nights or dragging the mattress in front of the TV on Sunday mornings to watch nature shows while eating your favorite breakfast.

Create fantasy and mystery. Pretend you are a stranger meeting at a designated place. Kiss in a dark narrow street. Enact a sexual fantasy—with you as the main dish.

Be glamorous. Share drinks and food in bed, with him dressed in the sexy underwear you bought him and you dressed in something soft and thin that can be easily removed.

Be exotic. Imagine you are on a Greek island … at a lonely café or bar … on a pier jutting into the sea … with candles gently flickering … and the clink of crystal glasses merging with the light sounds of Vivaldi's *Four Seasons* wafting through the heavens … as fishing boats inch across a dark crimson seascape … into a panorama of misty isles … You get the picture!

Be elaborate. Be his servant for the night. Possibly his slave. Shop for food and drink, and cook an elaborate meal. Tack a menu outside the door for his arrival. When he walks in hand him a glass of champagne and soak his feet in a basin of soothing warm water as prep for a foot massage. After the massage, a taste of sherbet. He's your king and you are his slave—perhaps his birthday gift.

Traveling is always romantic. Bed-and-breakfast … smothering him with kisses.

Affection is romantic. Kiss him when you wake up and when you go to bed.

Let him know he's your hero. Listen to his stories of conquest with obvious admiration. Every once in a while tell him you are proud of him. He wants to be your hero.

Gifts. Give him fantasy. It costs very little.

Be curious. Love is an exploration!

Small kindnesses are low hanging fruit. They're so easy! A big hello and a smile to start the day—or anytime.

Touch him. Males need to be touched 2 or 3 times more frequently than females to attain the same level of satisfaction according to a study by Swedish researcher Kerstin Unas-Moberg. A spontaneous hug is so cool!

Have his back. Lovers Jamie and Eddie on the TV series Blue Bloods had written and memorized the following for their engagement vow. "I will always have your back. If you fall behind

I will wait up. I'll earn your respect, and pay you respect, every day we have. I'll be your scout, your night watchman, your cavalry, your medic… your chaplain in our army of two. No retreat. No surrender. You can count on me.

Remember: Plan ahead and Set the mood! (Notice in the beginning story of chapter 7 how she plans ahead and sets the mood). And practice, practice!

What Works for Guys

Insert romantic ideas into a "Romance Cheat Sheet" in your phone. Plan ahead, set the mood, and Practice! Practice!

9. Intimacy = Truth + Trust

About Intimacy

Intimacy can be defined variously as close familiarity, or friendship, companionship, a cozy private atmosphere, or an act of love. My friend, Barney, confided in me that intimacy is "sharing stories and life episodes so another feels they have seen the world through our eyes." Another friend, Leszek, would say intimacy means "see into me."

I believe there are two fundamental types of intimacy. The first, I call *ravaging intimacy,* otherwise known as falling-in-love. This majestic intimacy between two people causes sparks to fly. Every inducement nature has conjured up comes into play — attraction of opposites, pheromones, oxytocin, dopamine — to make you want to ravage the other, all the time. These sparks are so powerful, that they forged the very existence of our species. Lust grabs control of our brain and directs eager fingers to caress, eyes to adore and explore, olfactory glands to smell delicacy, ears to translate sweet nothings into complements or crucial communication, and the heart to pound hot blood into our genitals until they beg for relief. Every part of our body and soul seems to be into the other. Even our kisses convey, through billions of cells, the degree to which this other person is compatible and desirable. If those ravaging feelings last long enough to evolve into true love, we become soulmates and travel through time together. Oh, how sweet is this intimacy! "See into me, please. I love you so."

The second type of intimacy is everything–else that constitutes "see into me," for instance, knowledge of family history, how one was brought up, their sexual tendencies, likes, beliefs, behavior, past love affairs, feelings, and the thoughts formally withheld because of disinterest, fantasies, fears, all the things that make a person who they are. This kind of intimacy shared with another person often proves to be the most durable. "I trust enough to tell another my truth, without fear of reprisal." And the other does the same. I can become the kind of guy a woman with an exceptional toothy-smile and sparkling eyes jumps on and wraps her legs around when I arrive, the kind of person she would call *my friend.* We are interested in what each other says, whether with enthusiasm or pain. We ask questions. *Everything-else intimacy* makes us truly alive. We have the opportunity to be someone's soulmate who is not our lover. Why can't friends and selected family be soulmates?

Observations

* There is a purity about intimacy, a freshness that never seems to fade.

* Women seem to have an easier time than men creating and sharing intimacy. The how-tos are probably passed on in their genes. This knack, however, can also open men up to be "seen." I especially like the intimacy between mother and daughter as it is reflected in the old classic movie, ***Terms of Endearment***: each individual overcomes the age barrier to expose private thoughts, trusting that the other will listen without reprisal, and rather, with heart-felt emotion. Compare that sense to my friend Rich's sentiments. He said, "I abhor the dishonesty in hiding what I really feel, but hate the conflict that results from exposing my inner feelings."

* It's clear that intimacy increases with the ability to truthfully express your feelings. That's why I believe men are critically short of intimacy. This shortage seems to become more acute as they age, when intimacy dissipates into brief unemotional conversations, lack of contact, or occasionally sent emails or messages that rarely extend past one paragraph and convey little. I've asked women whether their husbands or boyfriends have friends. They invariably answer, "Oh, yes, lots of them." When I follow up with,

"What if he has a problem with your relationship? Who does he talk to?" The most frequent response is, "I've been trying to get him to make a friend he can really talk to!"

* Intimacy is often easy with people we don't know, and so hard with people we do know. For instance, intimacy with random travelers was the very best feature of my years traveling. Travelers have no axe to grind. They trust you are telling the truth, and are non-judgemental about what that truth conveys. There's no ego to feed or defend against. Travelers "see into" you.

* Intimacy is as difficult to maintain as an aging athlete's edge on competition. The aging ego often seems to shun intimacy. Come on, people! Intimacy is whipped cream on the pie of life. It is beautiful truth conveyed to a trusting person.

Story: *On an island in Thailand, a handsome, dark, young Australian man was trying to define intimacy by describing the closest thing to it he could remember. "She was in her early forties," he said, "married for about 20 years and in an aging relationship with problems. Then I come along—young, muscular and honest. She was the mother of my best high school friend. I felt fatally attracted to her, as if I'd known her before. I was 18 and a virgin.*

"We were alone in her vacation house by pure chance, mate, and I spilled it all. I confessed I was in love with her and felt bloody miserable. She gave me a Mona Lisa smile I'll never forget. First, she asked me a lot of questions about myself. Then she took my hand and, without words, led me into her bedroom. She closed the door but left a light on so we could see each other. She was gentle, yet hungry. I still remember the smell of her lavender perfume that evening, mate. After that connection, I never saw her again."

"What a wonderful way to lose your virginity," I said. "From another perspective you related your innermost feelings to her. You were honest and she trusted you because you were truthful. When you think about it, honesty seems like the ultimate intimacy."

What about you? Do you want intimacy? Can you overcome the truth-trust conundrum to feel its tenderness? First let's check out the conundrum.

10. Truth-Trust Conundrum

It takes two to speak the truth—one to speak, the other to hear. —Henry David Thoreau

A friend's revelation

Story: *"My most intimate discussion with my wife came after 10 years of marriage. We discussed openly and honestly our experiences and intrigue with the opposite sex. At the beginning of our marriage, we had no illusions about whether we would have sex with someone else during the entire course of our marriage, forever. Forever is a long time! We intellectually discussed infidelity in the early years, without judging each other. But it wasn't until one fateful night, when the truth leaked out and our egos were bruised, that we faced our innermost feelings. We literally locked into each other, mentally and sexually, exposing details of our extramarital sex. Only then did we achieve soul-to-soul intimacy and the feeling that we could share anything."*

<u>**The conundrum:**</u> Is it wise to tell the truth (as in, "I had a very sweet fling with Jolinda, but it didn't mean a thing?") to someone who is likely to hit you over the head with a mallet and distrust you for ever after.

Michael Connelly, prolific author of books about the American criminal justice system, writes on the first page of ***The Last Coyote:*** "Everybody lies. Cops lie. Lawyers lie. Witnesses lie. Victims lie. A trial is a contest of lies … The judge knows this. Even the jury knows this …" Would Connelly's world of liars exist to the extent he says if people truly heard us? Thoreau put truth on an elegant perch, didn't he?

What about listeners? How many relationships could be saved if the offended party, who otherwise would be lied to, dispensed with their ego and asked, "Why did you do it?" Then listened to the answer, and discussed that answer with suspended judgement?

The truth about truth is that fear of reprisal, misunderstanding, manipulation, embarrassment and the weaknesses of others, such as low self-esteem, having to be right and control-addiction, all work against telling truth. We fib to kids all the time because we think they can't handle truth. Politicians lie about affairs for fear their family can't handle truth. Men lie to get into women's pants and women lie to avoid being wrong. News and social media arrange truth to satisfy their audience's demand for their brand of truth and drama. CNN's liberalism and Fox News's conservatism, for example, make money on your biases, which have become their brand. They interview people according to the truth they want to present to you, their listeners. That's what we want, right? Often, we, the people, lie or conveniently avoid correcting a statement we know to be false to avoid getting hammered with horrific emotions like: "I want a divorce." "You broke what we had!" "I don't want to hear that!" "You ruined my life!" "You broke my heart!"

"Beauty is truth. Truth is beauty." Keats knew that truth is like a rare flower—beautiful and illusive—because truth takes trust.
If truth is beauty, then trust is its creator.

Everyone is their own universe. Our reality and values are not necessarily others' reality and values. Differences are ubiquitous. However, Trust is the common denominator that makes different universes work in harmony. Trust binds friendships, marriages, business partnerships, orchestras and bands, executive staffs in business and family. If trust is not in your relationship, your relationship probably will not work in the long term. So, those who purchase cell phone spy programs to discover if their loved one cheated would be better off quitting the relationship.

Story: *While I was enjoying Indonesian dining with a young American couple I met on Gilly Meno, a tiny island not far from Bali, an elegant woman from Australia appeared as if from nowhere. As she climbed the outdoor restaurant's creaky wooden stairs, an island breeze gently directed the folds of her long white lace beach gown. "Hi," she said, with fresh effervescence, as if she knew us, "My name is Joy." The four of us spent a lovely evening and left the restaurant singing a song of friendship. During the meal we decided to walk around the island the next day, which was New Year's Day.*

On the walk, we regularly changed partners so we had a chance to tell our stories to each other. The thing about travelers is that you can trust them to listen, usually without judgment. When it was my turn with Joy, she said she was escaping her hometown after having divorced her husband two years earlier, which was followed by suffering through a disastrous breakup with her subsequent boyfriend, the love of her life. He had seen an old girlfriend and Joy didn't believe him when he tried to explain that their meeting was innocent. She demanded that he leave. Later, she wrote him a letter to break off their engagement.

"He wrote a rather sensitive letter in reply," she said, wrinkling her nose, a prelude to tears, "saying we needed to trust each other. 'What else is love?' was the way he phrased it. And if I didn't trust him, what was the sense of carrying on?"

There are probably more stories involving mistrust then there are of trust. Take the famous story of John Wayne Bobbitt, for instance. At their home in Virginia in 1993, his wife, Lorena Bobbitt, manifested her deep-seated distrust due to his sex escapades by attacking him with a carving knife while he slept. She chopped off a section of his penis and threw it out the window into a field. Surgeons managed to reattach the retrieved penis. Lorena became a media star and John was able to function normally on his numerous subsequent dates. Lorena, now his former wife, was found not guilty of attacking her husband by reason of insanity.

Without this dark side of trust—or lack of trust—especially in third-party intrigue (where a third party manipulates through lies), Hollywood would go bust.

Make someone trustworthy: trust them. Do you trust the man in your life enough to:
- listen to him without interruption?
- believe what he is saying during an argument?
- discuss your feelings about him?
- hear about his strip-club experience?
- accept that he's trying to educate you, rather than verbally abuse you, when he points out what you consider a *fault* in you?

When pheromones fade and opposites irritate, trust reverses and issues become entombed. I call them zombies—habits that feed on distrust and pierce the heart during arguments. Self-esteem issues (deeply ingrained and burdensome), insecurity, previous negative experiences, faulty intelligence, misinterpretation of facts and a slew of differences invite distrust, not to mention messages that our confused genes toss at us, like "Don't trust men!"

Don't pamper zombies! You don't have to let go of your truth to understand somebody else's.

Story: During the summer break at Providence College, between my junior and senior years, I worked in Hampton Bays, New York, at the Canoe Place Inn. I did bookkeeping during the day and was manager of the hotel dining-theater at night. I started dating an attractive junior at Boston University who was one of 14 waitresses working for the restaurant that summer. To my everlasting delight, she taught me about sex. I usually stayed at the hotel during the week and went home on weekends. One Saturday, I walked into the house and my mother was waiting for me in the kitchen.

"Denis," she said quietly, "I need to speak to you."

This was a first. She rarely scolded me. For good reason, Mom trusted me. But clearly, she had a dilemma which I seemed to be the root of. I followed her through the kitchen, wondering what was going on, beyond the nanoscale food pantry and into the washroom. She pulled out one of my wrinkled jeans from a laundry bin next to the rusty old refrigerator. Then she dipped her hand into the right pocket and extracted, with distasteful reluctance, a condom.

"Do you know what this is?" she asked, conveying her discomfort. She felt obliged to confront me on this particular issue, but her appearance told me that she really didn't want to discuss it. Neither did I. How it got in my pocket was the question on my mind! The pants hadn't been washed yet, and she seemed honor-bound as a parent to proceed.

"I do, Mom. It's a condom. But I wouldn't worry if I were you."

"Why not?"

"Well, as you can see, it's ... not used."

"Thank heavens!" she said, relieved. She gave me the condom and placed the pants back in the laundry bin. "You know, Denis, you can talk to me anytime you want."

"Thanks, Mom. I'll keep that in mind." I walked away feeling that she trusted me. I was glad the secret discussion was over, as I am quite sure she was.

Trust is crucial in relationships, like business.

Story: *When I was a young executive manufacturing and selling leading-edge computers, I asked one of our board members, Bob Noyce, how long it had taken for his executive staff at Intel to function together as a team. Replying to my question after a moment of reflective thought, he said, "About two years. I think it takes most executive staffs about that long to trust each other. The sooner, the better, but there are some people who you can't rush."*

He used the word trust. Much later, when I had my own consulting firm, it took my partner, Larry Hill, and me that long to fully trust each other. Our business—fixing companies—required our clients to have a great deal of trust in us. But Larry and I had to work out jealousies, differences in experience and splitting partnership money. Looking back on our long-running partnership, we achieved an extraordinary level of trust and respect. Each of us fed the other. To my recollection we never argued. For over 20 years I shared with him one of the most unique experiences of my life. You trust—you don't fight. When he said something, I trusted that it was true and never thought he had some ulterior motive. Having trust allowed us to listen to each other the way Maslow described.

Trust prevailed over jealousy, certainly on my part, because Larry was an extraordinarily talented man. He was the strong, silent, intelligent type you know, with a wisp of silky brown hair dipping slightly over his forehead, who exploded into a delightful childlike laugh when he found something funny. We listened carefully to each oth-

er. Feelings of inadequacy or superiority that often creep into long-term relationships were simply not there after our initial adjustment period. We were each other's advocates because of trust, and could convey thoughts at important meetings with the most imperceptible movement of the eye.

Some of my relationships with women had confusing trust issues. They trusted me in general, but often not enough to listen. My past offenses or character flaws I'm sure. But I was fortunate to have mom and Larry who trusted me, just the way I was.

What Works for Guys

"Make someone trustworthy: trust him."
Henry Stinson

11. HELP! Resolving Conflict

"That's where relationships falter; they can't get beyond the hurtful. Someone usually shuts down about a real issue, and the other doesn't want to bring it up again for fear of a bloody confrontation. Issues linger." — The Traveler by Denis Hickey

Story: Some years back in Cairo, I heard a disturbance below my second-floor room. A vocal crowd of 12 men had surrounded two arguing dudes. Suddenly, friends pulled the combatants away from the fracas and two other men substituted for them, standing in their places. Using these proxies, the crowd discussed and disputed the issues. The original combatants watched and listened to what the crowd thought, occasionally throwing in their two cents. Not a bad approach!

Help!

The first step in solving any problem is to admit there is one. If you don't think there's a problem and he does, you could be the problem. Read the heat-of-battle comments below. If any of them are part of your dialogue, the two of you have a problem.

- "Listen to me! Try to empathize!"
- "Why talk? There's nothing I am going to say that you're going to accept!"
- "You're never wrong! All this is about you being right!"
- "Everything you're saying is an attack.
- "We repeat the same dynamic over and over!"

Two do-it-yourself approaches that may help resolve conflict. Both involve trust.

1. Compassion, as in Emotionally Focused Therapy (EFT)

Story: *"People are often afraid to open themselves up to getting slammed." My daughter, Shannon, was talking with me about how certain women in my life live predominantly in the present. She said aspects of the past might be too painful to resurrect because of my strong character. A friend once said to me, "Arguments are rooted in the past because of an accumulation of hurts." Shannon suggested that perhaps people who avoid past dynamics freeze up at the thought of an uncomfortable memory.*

"Many people are deathly afraid of conflict. If we are unable to come from a place of compassion with a person like that," she said, "then it's difficult to have constructive communication with them."

"Take me, for instance. When I have an argument with Tom I am either defending my actions or on the offense—angry with him. My response causes him to defend his actions. But—and this is important—when I get clear on what's going on underneath the layers of my anger, there is usually some fear or sadness there. When I can get present and verbalize my vulnerable place, he can sink into compassion for me. Then we move into a whole new area of communication."

She gave an example. "If we are hosting a party or packing for a trip, I usually become anxious and agitated as the event gets closer. I begin to feel overwhelmed and worry that we are not going to get everything done on time. By the day of the party, it's likely that I'm going to get pissed at him because he's not doing enough to help or he's doing something I don't want him to do. When I let him know I'm not happy with him, he immediately goes on the defensive and we get in a fight. Now, I try to get present with what is going on underneath— my anxiety and fear of not getting it all done. I explore that fear. What will happen if I don't get things done? I will be sad about how our house looks. I talk to Tom from this vulnerable place rather than from an agitated, angry place. His response? He wants to hug me and reassure me that everything will be okay. He asks what he can do to help.

"Getting to a vulnerable place is hard work for us and it's taken a lot of practice, initially with our therapist. We were doing a type of couples therapy called Emotionally Focused Therapy (EFT). Now we are making progress without our therapist. The risk, which has sometimes happened, is that Tom's or my vulnerability may trigger a reaction that isn't compassion.

"A while back, when we were working on this approach to communicating, Tom got present with his vulnerable feelings, and instead of responding with compassion, I got scared. I didn't want to see him vulnerable. Now, with practice, slowing the conversation and creating room to explore our feelings underneath, rather than reacting with anger, we get in touch with what's going on for us underneath the anger. When we get present to that, we can communicate our feelings without blaming the other person. It feels much more like constructive communication.

"It takes being vulnerable, a willingness to feel compassion towards the other person and letting go of blame. You don't need blame. The other person will naturally take responsibility for their piece because of the compassion they feel. It's hard work, but easier with coaching we got in EFT."

Shannon always seems to make sense. I mulled over this compassion approach for a moment before responding.

"What you're saying is that rather than pointing out sins of the past, which is devoid of compassion and probably not possible to address anyway, and particularly if a person is uncomfortable with the

pain of the past, stay present with compassion. Uncover underlying fears to resolve conflict."

"That's sort of sums it up, Pops."

I like the sound of what Shannon proposed. It allows the person who is not afraid of the past to stay in a timeframe that's comfortable for their partner—the present or future.

"That would be hard for me," I told her. "Compassion is not one of my strong suits. But it sounds like it makes a lot of sense. I'll give it a try."

I did, and it worked!

2. Commitment to Talk

First set the stage. Purchase a three-minute sandglass or a similar device.

Open the door "Is now a good time to talk, or can we schedule a conversation later? I have a concern about …"

Then exchange information. Use the sandglass. Each person gets 3 minutes of spillage to make their points. If you haven't exhausted the issue after 3 rounds of 3 minutes each. Stop! Resume the next day. You will find that, uninterrupted for 3 minutes, your thoughts become concise and less preachy.

As Shannon said, "It takes being vulnerable, a willingness to feel compassion towards the other person and letting go of blame …" Say how you feel and what you want, without ego, so the other person understands. Silence is not necessarily agreement. Say, "Help me understand how that made you feel," and ask questions to clarify and understand his/her perspective: "I hear you saying ____. Is that right?"

Tip: Use "I" in your statements. Above all, *listen*.

Story: *Arguments often seem to be of a relationship-busting nature. In the heat of an argument, I found myself sliding into a wormhole to reflect on consequences. "How do I want this to turn out?" was my primary thought. In that brief moment, reflecting on consequences, I asked myself, "Is this drama worth breaking up over?" The answer was **no**. Then why be so pissed at her? These two thoughts didn't solve the problem or stop the argument, but they allowed me to listen better and change the heat level.*

The trick to changing the heat level for me was finding that brief moment or opportunity to change the energy. Say something funny, perhaps, or give a friendly smile. Then try to look at it from her/his point of view. After all, people want to be listened to and understood before they are ready to try to understand you. As Shannon said, compassion begets compassion.

Solve the Problem. What do you want the future to be? Reach an agreement. If the issue persists, hunt for the sandglass again.

What Works for Guys

Solve the problem

12. Is Love a Secondhand Emotion?

Love is an exploration.

Love is not being able to say enough good things about him/her.

Love is giving.

"**Love** is a decision. Lust is a feeling. Love is more organized than lust. It needs a modicum of communication." —my friend, Frank Zolfo

The Prophet by Kahlil Gibran: "When **love** beckons to you, follow him, though his ways are hard and steep … And when he speaks to you believe in him, though his voice may shatter your dreams as the north wind lays waste the garden. For even as love crowns you, so shall he crucify you. Even as he is for your growth, so is he for your pruning. Even as he ascends to your height and caresses your tenderest branches that quiver in the sun, so shall he descend to your roots and shake them in their clinging to the earth … Love gives us naught but itself and takes naught but from itself. Love possesses not nor would it be possessed; for love is sufficient onto love …"

Has overuse and perhaps cruelty made love a secondhand emotion, as Tina Turner has been crooning for decades? Let's look at a few of love's stages. See where you fit in.

Falling in Love. An exploration—you explore his/her mind, wanting to know everything about him, and wanting him to explore you. You devour every kiss and search every nook and cranny of his lips and mouth. He wants to feel and examine the lines on the palm of your hand. Discover! Explore! Devour!

According to experts, critical thinking pathways in the brain shutdown while the brain accesses bonding chemicals like dopamine, estrogen, oxytocin and testosterone. This state usually lasts for roughly 6 to 8 glorious months.

In–Love. Passion is refined and characterized by a high weekly incidence of making love. The couple has that certain look together. You become soulmates.

Love–10 years later. A camera panning the audience at a pro basketball game spotlights couples kissing. Ten-year couples give pecks or quick touches to the lips. Can you still picture the man you fell in love with? How you felt when he first touched you? How his kisses tasted? Is his smell the same today? In the last month, have you asked him a penetrating question about himself? Does that one characteristic you fell in love with still exist— his smile, wit, looks, intelligence, charm, sense of humor? Do you care about him more than yourself? Would you watch a whole football or basketball game with him? Are you still soulmates?

Loving Friends. The San Francisco Chronicle announces that an athletic legend had a party with 300 of his closest friends. Contrast that with an old Indian saying: "A friend is someone with whom you have eaten a pound of salt." That's a lot of meals over a long time. True friendships exhibit trust and require time spent. Among friends frequent arguments are dangerous, and they can be recalled negatively in later years.

Long-term friendships seem to require a non–judgmental attitude. Fundamentally, unless asked for your advice, it helps to trust that he is doing the best he can.

Thought: Keeping friendships with men brings to mind the saying about old soldiers, "they never die, they simply fade away." Keeping contact with him is key to friendship longevity, but don't expect a lot of words. Hunter habits often cause a retreat into silence.

TV Love. Geraldo Rivera says to a clinically depressed-for-20-years woman slumped in a chair saying she wants to die, "We love you!" His audience repeats, heart-felt, "We love you!" Can you really love a person you don't know who's been depressed for 20 years and who wants to die? Sounds like a secondhand emotion.

Family Love. This kind of love is likely to be for people with whom you have eaten a pound of salt. Family members can be people you care about more than yourself, and their love is often more forgiving than with friends. Relationships with family members can be based on obligations or can take on the majesty of friendships.

Admirers' Love. Basketball players love their fans. This love often lasts only as long as the shine stays on. But hey, it's love. Guys hugging seems to be an improvement, don't you think?

We throw around love the way we play catch. "Here! Catch some of my love!" "Hey! You need a little love?" "Show him some love!" "Come on over. We have a special on love today." But, whatever type of love you have, it will require giving of yourself in order to last.

Story: *For couples, I particularly enjoyed and admired a set of three movies starring Ethan Hawke (Jesse) and Julie Delpy (Celine):* ***Before Sunrise, Before Sunset*** *and* ***Before Midnight****. Each film explores the love affair between Jesse and Celine, two highly intelligent and attractive people. The three movies take place over 20 years. They are not action-packed go-go movies for the in-a-hurry or testosterone-driven crowd. They are cerebral. They contain magnificent dialogue between the two lovers who draw in their soul-mate through humor, jest and a mutually intelligent grasp and articulation of life-issues.*

Before Sunrise *has Jesse and Celine meet in their early 20s on a train to Paris. Not wasting a bit of youthful flirtation, they fall in love* and promise to reunite the next year in Paris, on a certain day on a certain bridge. As if to test fate they don't exchange personal information, like phone numbers. The movie's dialogue occurs in simple settings, such as on a train, in a quaint restaurant in a small French town, on a grassy, green hillside, at the train station where she leaves him for 10 years—perfect scenery for the smart, patient dialogue that leads two young people to the promised land. **It goes without saying that the saliva they swap has their subconscious activity working its full 90%, analyzing DNA for health and compatible procreation purposes.** They pass the test!

Ten years later, **Before Sunset** is released. Finally reunited in their early 30s, they spend another day discussing their adult lives to date. Jesse's in Paris, the best-selling author of a book about the most important day of his life, which was 10 years earlier in France. Celine notices his advance publicity in the local paper and surprises him during his reading at her favorite bookstore. The dialogue is romantic, at times intense and fun. They cautiously but provocatively talk about their lives, politics, love affairs, how the affairs never matched up to their karmic single day 10 years ago, and, finally, why they didn't meet on the Paris bridge the following year. For the second time, their bonding chemicals infect each other. They do not kiss, but they are falling in love for good—he misses the plane back to America and his family.

Before Midnight, the third movie, is bittersweet. It's about aging love. Now married with twin daughters, and with Jesse's son visiting from America, they have been together for 10 years, each having sacrificed parts of their previous lives to share a multicultural life together. They are vacationing at a seaside resort. After dinner with friends, it's just the two of them, hoping to spend a night of passion. But the night turns into a test of their relationship and a discussion of what their future holds. Deep-rooted resentment—the kind that inevitably builds up in long-term relationships—makes this movie the most emotional of the series. There is truth and fiery honesty in a story of true love—the kind of love that **The Prophet** describes in *the quote at the beginning of this chapter. A romance with swooning highs and familiar lows—fights, jealousy and tests of wills between the emotion of women and analytical nature of men. In the end, trust and memories of what it took to find each other prevail. They clash, they compromise, they make love.*

The iTunes summary of one of Ethan Hawke's movies describes his real life persona, in which he identifies as a feminist and has criticized "the movie business [for being] such a boys' club." Hawke has repeatedly denounced the overemphasis on the importance of monogamy: "People have such a childish view of monogamy and fidelity. 'He's cheated so he's bad, she's cheated so she's bad,' as opposed to a recognition that our species is not monogamous. Sexual fidelity can't be the whole thing you hang your relationship on. If you really love somebody, you want them to grow, but you don't get to define how that happens. They do."

Love doesn't have to become a secondhand emotion. As The Prophet indicates, love is pleasure and difficulties and responsibilities wrapped in one package. Love is giving. If you really love him, and you need to pull away from sex with him for whatever reason, would you want him to still be happy by enjoying sex with someone else?

What Works for Guys

Cherish that one thing you love about him. Yours truly cherishes her smile for me.

13. Weary Relationships

Nothing ventured, nothing gained.

My wife's uncle, celebrating his 50th wedding anniversary, told me his marriage had lasted because of tenacity and not having any serious financial problems. He had been fortunate. How many couples have no serious financial problems? But shouldn't tenacity carry us forward? And if this is so, how does a couple shake off relationship weariness and rearrange their existence to insert fun and love back into play? Let's start at the beginning.

Young people. Committing to someone when young is probably the biggest decision a person makes in their lifetime. Big decisions should involve time and study. Think about differences, as discussed in the first three chapters, and whether you can survive them. If possible, make real wedding vows based on what you can commit to achieving. Marriage is far too important for you to make traditional platitudes the basis of lifelong promises. Later, long after the attraction of opposites and pheromones wear off, doesn't it make sense to rethink the situation and compose new vows aimed at renascence? To rekindle what you had by changing what you can and accepting what you can't change. It takes commitment, courage and risk to adjust midstream, but happy people do it all the time.

Story: *Six months after his 24th birthday and four months before his wedding, my friend Stefan's fiancée arranged for the parish priest to conduct a Pre-Cana conference, just for the three of them. It was standard procedure in those days. The conference was designed to determine if the man and woman were compatible and could handle Catholic marital doctrine. She and Stefan talked for three hours with the middle-aged priest, discussing their personality types, hopes and dreams, family, sex and a variety of topics including attitudes towards religion. Afterwards, the priest was candid. "I'm not sure why you two are getting married," he said. "You don't seem to have much, if anything, in common."*

She burst out sobbing. "I bought my dress, and so did the bridesmaids. And we already sent out wedding invitations!"

Stefan told me later that inwardly he had been thinking exactly what the priest voiced, but he'd kept his mouth shut, patted her on the back and said, "Don't worry about what he said, Sweet Pie. We're getting married." Down deep, where he didn't want to go, he had a foreboding feeling.

A year later, in the midst of an argument, she blurted out, "I don't know why we ever got married! We have nothing in common! I don't like your friends. You don't like mine … I want a divorce!" So they cut their losses and got out early.

I know it's a strange thing to say, but she made them both happy in the long run. They didn't fit together. Stefan told me he had never been so happy as when she dumped him. He said that after the split they became good friends and now they meet once a year.

I like the idea of a priest or other qualified person counseling prior to marriage. Better yet, prior to engagement. My daughter thinks people should have counseling before they get married to get more bang for the buck, and in my book **The Traveler,** my friend, Frank Zolfo, lists 5 considerations for premarital counseling:

1. Do the couple accept each other for who they are, and acknowledge bad habits?
2. Are they committed to each other's dreams, and to empowering each other to achieve them?
3. Can they communicate vulnerability without it being used against them, and can they live through bad times?
4. Will they make good parents? Did they consider each other's genes, take a hard look at each family culture and have a joint philosophy on raising kids with a clear view of the role of religion?
5. Do they have similar interests? (I would add: a perspective on creative sex to stimulate slow times, a loyalty pledge focused on trust and an occasional joint.)

Again, the problem: What young couple is going to be practical when emotions run the show? However, worded properly, these considerations might be valuable criteria, for the discerning person, to screen for Mr. Right while using online dating applications.

Contract period. Each relationship has its lifetime–its contract period, so to speak: love affair, marriage, business relationship, friendship. In previous generations, marriage was forever. Parents, grandparents, aunts, uncles and cousins helped a couple fulfill their "till death do us part" agreement. Then the drive for gender equality in America and elsewhere caused a staggering rise in the divorce rate (in the US, from 20% in the 1950s to over 50% in the 1980s). Divorce rates have recently been dropping because couples wait longer to marry or live together and split without marrying, and there is a greater acceptance of single-parent households. Still, marriage is not guaranteed "for life." We need to cultivate marriage.

When you start a marriage today, there is still a strong chance you're going to divorce. Like any good partnership agreement, working out the terms of a divorce in advance would be infinitely better than working them out in the heat of battle. But that's hardly going to happen. A marriage contract today lasts as long as the spouses are fair and considerate, have physical, emotional and/or financial desire for each other, or as long as they are resigned to misery. If these elements come undone, the contract ends.

Weary relationships

Differences between people make most relationships weary with time. I can't imagine how they wouldn't. There are plenty of suggestions in this book and my first book in this series, *How to Make a Woman Happy,* to turn around a weary relationship, so long as the couple has commitment.

There is little intimacy in a weary relationship. Instead, there is an overwhelming sense of not being heard and the feeling that each partner is not interested in what the other says. Sex is mechanical or absent, one partner or both are selfish, body smell has changed, and there is often friction caused by sour finances.

When your relationship is weary or downright miserable, the contract has probably expired and you have three alternatives:
1. Commit to fix what's broken.
2. Move on to greener pastures, alone or with someone else.
3. Keep suffering.

If you want to make him happy, and yourself, only the first and second choices are available. Fixing anything takes desire to change, commitment, courage and risk. If you are willing to commit to working on the problem, rip out the past to breathe fresh air. Then start to reseed the garden. Otherwise, make yourself and maybe some other man happy by moving on. Sure, change is uncomfortable and risky, but the biggest risk to happiness is doing nothing. ***Nothing ventured, nothing gained.***

Fixing what's broken requires change, and the key to successful change is visualizing the future you want to live together. Then ask yourself, "what change will be required for both of us to have that future?" Visualizing, of course, means calling on the future time frame for assistance. Start with a statement, not exceeding 15 words, that spells out what you want to achieve together. For instance," I want us to be good friends and share intimate times again." That's 12 words. It's easy to remember! If you put energy into that particular future, weariness has a chance of fading away. Visualize who you want to be, and live that future–now!

Zodiac signs are a good way to think about relationship compatibility as a prelude to fixing what's broken. According to astrology-zodiac-signs.com, "Two people whose zodiac signs are highly compatible will get along very easily because they are on the same wavelength. But people whose zodiac signs are less compatible, will need to be more patient and tactful in order to achieve a happy and harmonious relationship."

Check the Compatibility Love Chart, below, to grasp the extent of your need to be patient and tactful. Simply locate your zodiac sign in the left column and read across to find the size of the heart located in the column that corresponds to your partners zodiac sign. The bigger the heart, the higher your compatibility.

As a Leo - with my wife being a Virgo - I've had the benefit of glorious passion, to the maximum - thanks to opposites attracting. After all, opposites attracting provided the expanded tool-chest for our very survival as a species. But, in the long run, when the hormones wore off and our differences began to clash, I needed patience, tact, commitment and occasional humility to mitigate the inevitable flying sparks. I have not always been successful at mitigating my shortcomings, I'm afraid, and we've had tough times along with the passion, but I suppose we will forever be working at fixing and improving. I guess that's what *The Prophet* referred to in the introduction to chapter 12, when he said:

"for even as love crowns you, so shall he (the "love") crucify you. Even as he is for your growth, so is he for your pruning. Even as he ascends to your height and caresses your tenderest branches that quiver in the sun, so shall he descend to your roots and shake them in their clinging to the earth."

Compatibility Love Chart
Source: Astrology-zodiac-signs.com

Thoughts:

- **Back to having fun.** Try the 3 to 1 approach. Say 3 good things about him to every criticism. If you're not sure what he considers a criticism, ask him.
- **Remember** good memories from the past.

Greener Pastures: if you are considering the second option through divorce, you might want to consider surrounding yourself with unbiased advisers who know your partner - preferably, both male and female. Also, to plan a harmonious approach to your future, think about your astrological compatibility and seek to understand your differences. Try to remember how you felt about him early on in your relationship. By softening harsh emotions, you can replenish a little trust and decrease the amount of heartache and grief inherent in divorce.

Story: *Before she got divorced, my friend, Althea relied on four advisors, three of whom had already been divorced. Those three friends gave advice based on their own marriages, which had ended miserably.*

"Close the bank accounts and take the money," one said.

"Don't contact him or let him bully you with words," said another.

The fourth advisor, married happily, mixed realism and compassion. She said, "You left him, Althea, and he's pissed. Whoever leaves should be kinder and gentler. You said he's not talking to anyone, and that his mom talks to you and his dad doesn't talk to anybody. He has no intimate friends with whom to share his misery. But you don't live with him anymore. When he calls and he's angry, hold the phone away from your ear. Humor him in a nice way. What does it cost you? You say he's not doing what needs to be done for the divorce, that it's moving at the pace of a glacier. He's a Leo and an engineer! Give him a list!"

Althea held the phone away from her ear when her ex was frustrated and wanted to take it out on her. No problem. She'd left him! She gave him a to-do list of jobs to finish around the house, to-dos with their child and to complete the divorce. The to-do list worked—of course! He's an engineer!

I also liked the friend's use of the zodiac. I have found over the years that zodiac signs and astrological readings can be surprisingly accurate. When a friend or family member has a newborn, I have my virtuoso, Susanne, do such a reading for the child with its new family. It's a great gift and unique way to welcome the little one into the world.

The end of the story is that while Althea and her ex are not friends now, they work well together with their daughter, and his animosity has faded.

Break-up stories. Each relationship has its story and storyteller. Women often tell the break-up story, so be fair—like Althea. Understand his point of view and how his differs from yours.

What Works for Guys

- You are who you were meant to be, but you can adjust.
- 3 to 1 approach. Say 3 good things about him to every criticism.

14. Intimacy with Dads and Husbands

Premise: Families with the strongest connection between mother and father are happier. Logic: if the parents are happy, the kids have an atmosphere of happiness in which to grow, and therefore a better chance of being happy themselves.

Do you have intimate moments with Dad? By raising kids and being dad, a man can create wonderful memories. I remember my youngest, Sean, talking on the phone when he was three, just before we traveled from Warsaw to the US. "We're flying to Florida, Grandma. I'll call you in a few minutes when we get back." At age two, my daughter, Chimene, wearing a floppy hat that nearly covered her eyes and my wife's woman-size galoshes, grabbed a plastic bat that was longer than her entire body, stood up and swung at a ball. My oldest daughter, Shannon, handed me a glass of wine and told me she was sooo proud to have a father she could talk to—before laying on me that she had lost her virginity!"

I guess when you get down to basics, families are about supporting each other and raising well-adjusted children. Researchers have found that children of fathers who played roughly (not in a negative way) were the most self-confident in adolescence and achieved close connections with older males later in life. They have also found that children whose fathers disciplined them were rewarded with better grades, higher education, and fewer behavioral problems. Girls who had a close relationships with dad got along better with men later in life.

But how do husbands and dads fare in this support process? Who teaches us to be dad? Way, way back, the hunter's job was to create, protect, and provide. After creation, he provided food, security and, hopefully, a favorable place in the clan's pecking order. In return, the hunter received fulfillment of his sexual desires, companionship and, if lucky, intimacy and the satisfaction of raising good kids. Still, our hunter heritage, encapsulated in every one of our incredible number of cells, may not include much of a background for realizing intimacy within family.

Given the number of instructions in the female's extra "X," intimacy has to be a no-brainer benefit. She's a gatherer. She's got girlfriends. She emotes. Females could teach men, delicately of course, the ins and outs of intimacy. In tune with that concept, I'd like to throw out, for discussion, a couple of touchy family-related situations from a man's point of view. Keep in mind that my male brain and my own universe is totally different from a woman's, by nature. As a result, I may articulate these situations differently than you might think proper. But trust me! My premise is that understanding dad and husband will assist you in helping him be the best he can be.

After baby arrives

Dr. Brizendine says that for "a new mother, being glued to her child, body and soul, alters her brain, because **the more you do something, the more cells the brain assigns to that task.**" She says "pregnancy followed by the stress of caring for baby causes a mother to lose an average of 700 hours sleep in the first postpartum." She further says that hormones shut off mom's desire for sex, that her new love and breast-feeding replaces or interferes with her desire for her partner, because the positive feelings she gets from sexual intercourse are met by meeting basic needs of her children. "The doctor further describes how "oxytocin and dopamine with baby make her feel loved, deeply bonded, and physically and emotionally satisfied."

It's helpful to look at a hunter's mind at this point. What happens to hunter/hero/lover when she switches her lover and drops sex out of her top 10 to-dos after the first postpartum? Sure, he's happy about the baby and concerned about her. What dad/husband wouldn't be? He and his wife did it! He's a dad now. As time passes, that jubilation only partially mitigates his own deprivation, but he doesn't quite understand what's happening. She is his soulmate, right? Intimacy and sex are intertwined in his universe, right? But what happened to sex? With the combination of society's reluctance to talk about sex, his ignorance of the hormonal changes dictating his life, and her 700 hours of lost sleep, an enlightened discussion between spouses is out of the question. Sorry, buddy! Mom's got a new lover!

The Masai tribe, a much older society than ours, understood and honored the socio-biology of mom and dad.

Story: *The adventurer, Henry Stanley, said to a 19th century London audience: "If there are any ladies or gentleman this evening who are specifically desirous of becoming martyrs, I do not know in all my list of travels where you could become martyrs so quickly as in Masai."*

A friend had arranged for me to have dinner with Ole Kina in Nairobi when I was there. Ole Kina had recently passed the Kenyan bar exam, no small feat for the son of a Masai cow herder who grew up in a small dusty hut in the savanna. I was excited at the prospect of spending time with a member of the tribe that had fascinated me as a young adult. I dressed in a bright blue shirt with orange flowers connected by blood-red vines and yellow dots. Swirling white lace embroidered the shirt hem and neck. African colors, not to be compared with my business attire back home.

"This is your chance to pump him about Africa," my friend teased as we arrived at a bar featuring a butcher shop at the entrance. Hefty beef slices, pestered by lazy flies, dangled from hooks. Four men waited at the meat stand. She introduced me to Ole Kena, whose blue-

striped suit and white shirt barely contained his handsome 6-foot-2 frame, with shoulders so broad he appeared to be wearing football pads inside his suit jacket. Ole, in turn, introduced his equally tall and wiry elder brother, John, and two friends, Kuto, an accountant, and Robert, an economist with Barclays Bank, who was short in comparison to the others. All were Masai in their mid-20s, save Robert whose Kikuyu tribe dominated politics in Kenya at the time. Introductions made, my friend politely split to attend other chores.

Ole chose a large slab of dangling red beef, and the butcher wrapped it in newspaper. I was relieved to note that it was the reddest meat in the stall. Red indicated healthy to me. Then we entered the dimly lit, dank-smelling bar and seated ourselves at one of 15 or so stark wooden tables. Half the tables were empty, and the others were occupied by black men and women sitting and quietly sipping drinks. There was no music.

Once seated, Ole Kina ordered a round of Tusker beer and handed the meat wrapped in newspaper to the waiter. He explained in Queen's English, "One simply brings the beef into one's favorite bar; the barman cooks it over coals and delivers it to one's table."

Waiting for the cooked chunks and french fries to arrive, we drank beer and discussed how to bleed cows and mix the blood with warm milk squeezed from the cow's utter, the tribe's daily staple of protein on the Savannah. The barman placed a large pile of cooked beef chunks on our table and poured a pyramid of salt and a pile of French fries next to the beef. We picked at the fries, dipped chunks in salt and munched while we talked. Scrumptious! The food was devoured during discussions about, among other subjects, democracy; economic slavery in light of Africa's massive debt; the International Monetary Fund; the Masai's divine right, as chosen people, to own all the Earth's cattle; when each of us lost our virginity; male circumcision in front of the tribe as a rite of passage into manhood; and polygamy.

"Tell me about polygamy?" I asked, loving the nature of this conversation.

> *"I can only answer for the Masai,"* Kuto replied. *"Marriage among us is often arranged, and is for the purpose of having children. You see, the number of children determines a man's security in old age. Polygamy, you ask? A man can have several wives, depending on his wealth."* He looked at me with furrowed brow, as if he'd just noticed a missing link— *"How many wives do you have?"*
>
> *"One,"* I answered. Then, hesitating while wondering if he was having fun with me, *"Isn't one enough?"*
>
> They all laughed. *"Maybe you are wiser than the Masai,"* Robert joked.
>
> Kuto continued. *"We are polygamists out of respect for women, to give them time between children. A Masai cannot have intercourse with his wife when she is pregnant or when she is nursing. He marries other women to fill his need and to increase the size of his family."*
>
> After dinner, the guys walked me safely back to my guesthouse, my mind spinning with the educational and controversial nature of our conversation, and the charm and fun I was enjoying. It occurred to me at the time that this very old Masai tribe respected the natural needs of both mother and father, with actions which would be inappropriate, and indeed illegal, in my own society.

Should we pay heed to the Massai and make a few adjustments to the way we think about sex? Like understanding and respecting male and female sexual needs at a more sophisticated level. The Masai family premise articulated by these young men, that children take care of parents when they age—the pension plan—has changed in modern societies that have adopted public pension plans. But the need for sex has not changed in our mostly monogamous habits. It seems to me that, in our society, talking about sex and learning about hormones and sexual differences to understand our own nature is crucial to avoid the needless sulking and damage to relationships that occurs during pregnancy and post-childbirth. Why is talking about sex so difficult, anyway? There could be a sweet intimacy to this discussion, which would turn her confusion and his anger and feeling of rejection into compassion.

Kids versus the Couple

Kids enhance families, not necessarily relationships. People I know without kids seem to have an easier time being companions. Kids can create jealousies and conflict. More variables to deal with, I guess. When I go to dinner at a restaurant, I like to survey the scene. Here's what I have observed time and again:

There is invariably a table of three. Mom, a young child in a baby seat to her right, and Dad. Early on, dad talks to mom and child, perhaps kidding and laughing. As the meal progresses dad begins to withdraw as mom pays more and more attention to the child. She goggles, instructs, laughs with the child and cuts its food. Dad looks lonesome and then bored. He's out of the loop.

The next time you're at a party with couples and their children, try to notice the interplay. At first the genders are mixed and talking to each other. The kids are playing. Before long, men are talking to men and women are talking to women. The men—the less sociably capable hunters—eventually struggle for subjects to discuss. Some stand around looking stranded. The women, meanwhile, have no struggle socializing. They're talking about kids and food—they're gatherers. After all, inside and out of the womb, she supplied the child with food, love and warm tummy rubs. Mothers and their children are simpatico.

Of course, the intimacy existing between a couple naturally switches to mom and the newborn! Most dads tell me they went from number one in her heart to what seemed like number three or four after a baby was born. It's not surprising, women bond with their baby and other women (Mom, sister who is a mother, etc.). A subtle replacement for him has come, along with the severe decline in sex. Maybe dad, feeling left out and unfulfilled, subconsciously withholds intimacy as a result. Who knows? How would you feel being replaced?

Story: *My mom used to say, in an exaggerated tone that mixed exasperation with incredulity, "Your father was in competition with his sons! He was jealous of them!" When she first said this, I let it pass, not thinking about what was really going on. Mom and Dad rarely got along, anyway. When I grew older, married with kids, I began to feel that mom had missed something important. It was only after experiencing the change from being first in my wife's heart, to second or third that I grasped my mother's naïveté, and my own, regarding my father's behavior. She had four sons and a daughter. Being a good mother and supplier for our welfare, she had a lot on her plate, and I'm sure she loved the kids more than she loved my father.*

Guys often joke about their post-baby sex life. But it's no joke. It's humbling and sad for us. My father had good reason to be jealous. With five kids, he went from numero uno to number six on her list. An only child himself, he had to have been even more jealous than those who had grown up in a large family. I remember losing that wonderful intimacy with my wife after the children arrived. Not understanding what was happening created frustration and anger, and resulted in a bit of a downward spiral in our relationship.

I can sympathize, but I can't empathize with what women go through after childbirth. I'm a guy! I can't feel the exhaustion a woman feels with the requirements of motherhood (preparing food, feeding, bathing, changing, rocking, dressing, especially for winter, getting up late at night, the incredible loss of sleep, the decline of testosterone and, with it, the declining desire for sex and resulting guilt). But I can possibly cut out the last item. Here's how.

Mothers, keeping in mind hubby's wiring and needs as a guy, remembering how he supplied intimacy when you needed it most, pre-and post-childbirth, how patient he was for you to come back to him, and how he was replaced as numero uno in your heart… now this may be crude, but give him a lusty hand job or better when you don't feel like going the whole nine yards. His limited instructions tell him to spread seed. What's a hand job versus the release and joy he receives? Love is giving, no? You get intimacy from the child. And dad?

Sex is fun and brings out the best in guys. Stop the fun for too long after the baby arrives at your own peril. Joe Quirk made this last point: "All this extra sex; all these extra erogenous zones; all this extra courtship; all this prime brain real estate devoted to foreplay; what is the point? To preserve the family. Our oversized penises and breasts and myriad of perversions exist to assure that males babysit. **The best way to save the family is to celebrate creative sexuality."** This makes sense to me.

Sex with him is low hanging fruit to his happiness. Remember, the penis is a muscle that needs exercise, or it atrophies. So why not exercise it!

In the final analysis, my mom was right. Dad was in competition with his sons. He was jealous. Don't let your kids lose dad's affection because he feels alienated and jealous. Ask yourself: "Did I drop my man from number one? Can I communicate a little more sexually, because he deserves more?" He's your soulmate. Right?

Dads and Daughters

When I lived in California, I constantly heard stories of grown women who had been severely damaged by lack of warmth and care from their dad. Listening to or telling a secret, hugging and playing give all children warm feelings they should be able to share with their dads.

Story: Situated along a mile of magnificent rugged California coast, south of Monterey, lies Esalen, a paragon of philosophy and psychology. It's perched comfortably in green splendor on a Pacific cliff, which drops down to a surf that relentlessly pounds colossal steel-gray rocks. Hot tubs fed by natural springs invite intelligent discussion, and massage tables swept by warm ocean breezes prepare you for heaven. One day, before my massage training, which I started while trying to transform from businessman to traveler, I attended a workshop about fathers. Women and men painfully talked about the paucity of intimacy or contact with their dads. Most cried. I don't recall why I was there. Maybe because of my own father, with whom I can't remember having a reasonable conversation. My dad is a book unto himself.

As part of the workshop, men were assigned roles as fathers, and the women as their daughters. The daughter I play-acted with was in her late 20s or early 30s. She said she had been severely denied intimacy with her dad. It was easy to role-play Dad with her. She rewarded any amount of sensitive behavior and humor with love. I prided myself on being a great dad. Growing up I studied my father and developed an approach to being a father. You have to like young people to be a good dad. I raised two girls who I adore, and now I've got a guy. I believed as a young man that my girls would never take a backseat to anyone. And to my knowledge they haven't.

I tried to show this dad-daughter connection to my Esalen daughter. A look, a touch, humor, playfulness and listening—what it's like to have a good dad! She clung to me, uncomfortably at times, her hunger for approval boundless. I like being guru-ish, to a point. But I've always been uncomfortable with needy women, because the women in my family have been incredibly solid. She said her dad *would always turn away from her when he returned from work and that she rarely received his validation—rather, only irritation!*

How could you not feel for her? A smidgen of personal interest her way returned a pound of payback. My Esalen daughter left for home after a couple of days. I had time to tell her about good dads and how to encourage a man to be more attentive with his daughters if she had kids of her own.

After this experience I understood and could empathize with women affected by distance from their fathers. It's sobering. My aunt used to say that my grandmother (her mother) would put the kids to bed before my grandfather came home from work. My aunt felt deprived of his warm attention, so needed by a young or growing girl. I don't want to diminish my grandmother. She was always my hero. It was all probably due to the times and her penchant for orderliness.

Support your man to be intimate with his children. Talk to him about being a sensitive, intimate dad.

Divorce and the need for intimacy

Young people can be hard judges when it comes to their parents' divorce. They have no experience with what it means to keep up a long-term relationship and what's normal between men and women during divorce, because they have no experience with long-term, and to them, divorce means separation from the people they love. But in the end, blood is thicker than water. You can have only one biological dad and mom.

Story: When my younger daughter, Chimene, was in college, she invited me to a beach party in Santa Cruz, California, on that same Pacific coast. I remember sparks exploding from blazing logs in a fire and flickering into the night's darkness. College kids milled around the light and its warmth, drinking beer and laughing. During the evening, a young woman, Chimene's roommate, approached me and started to chat. She seemed troubled. I asked her what was on her mind. A little awkward at first, here is how the conversation progressed:

"It's about my father. He's changed!"

"In what way?" I asked, figuring I probably was about the father's age.

She stared out to sea for a minute before responding. Waves relentlessly strode forward, like a silent army.

"He's not himself."

"How's that?"

"He's become an alcoholic and a womanizer," she said with anger rising. "And he gets violent!"

She must see me as a father figure who could be trusted, I thought. "How much does he drink?"

"Every night when he gets home he has a martini."

I took a shot in the dark. "Are your mom and dad going through problems?"

Without a hitch she said, "Yes, I think they're getting divorced. No one has said anything to me or my sister, yet."

"Do they fight?"

"All the time. I hate it." Her sad brown eyes began to tear.

"And what about the womanizing?" I asked, pushing moist sand around with my toes.

"He has a girlfriend! He sees her all the time. I hate her."

"Has he ever been with another woman besides this woman and your mom?"

"No, not to my knowledge." Her response was thoughtful, with a smidgen of softness.

"How long have your parents been fighting?"

"It seems like forever!"

I felt for her. Her family was breaking up and she was helpless to do anything about it. Worse, there was a new woman on the scene.

"What about the violence?"

"He hit my sister!" She said hit with the gusto of a slap. The softness was gone.

"How often?"

"Twice!"

"Had he ever hit either of you before?"

"No, just those times he hit my sister. He's never hit me."

"Was it during a time when your parents were fighting?"

She thought for a moment, as if a new element or some additional information had been brought into play. It took a full minute for her to respond. *"Yes, how did you know?"*

"It was a wild guess. Listen, do you mind if I say something?"

"I wish you would. This has been bottled up inside of me for so long."

She looked at me with hope in her eyes. Pausing for a moment to look out across the limitless sea, I caught crystal waves curling and dropping in the darkness. In case you're wondering, discussions like this were normal for me in my job - people in trouble and hurting.

With a knowing tone, while trying not to sound patronizing, I said, *"One martini after a day's work and after arriving home to a household in turmoil doesn't seem like alcoholism to me. My brother-in-law polishes off a half quart of whiskey before 3 p.m. every day. He's an alcoholic."*

I waited. She looked connected. *"When I was a kid, we got the strap. Sounds like your dad reacted out of marital rage. Interrupting a fight between frustrated parents nearing divorce is like grabbing a bone from the mouth of a hungry wolf. You do it at your peril."*

The next observation needed more diplomacy. "And the other woman ... Men don't normally have a lot of intimacy in their lives. Sometimes when there's trouble at home, another woman is a safe harbor. You know what I mean? It's not uncommon for a lonely guy to become involved in a relationship with another woman when things at home are rocky. Who else would they talk to? Most men wouldn't subject their kids to that pain. Your father was married for over 20 years, judging by your age. That's not trivial. He probably needed intimacy when he felt that he was losing his family."

I searched her eyes. She didn't seem to mind my devil's advocate role. Maybe that was why she had singled me out. My age and her roommate (my daughter) probably presented me as somebody who might understand her predicament.

"What's really bothering you?" I queried.

She suddenly burst out sobbing. Time passed. "My father was my best friend. Now I hardly see him! I blame him! I hate him! He's with her. I don't blame him about my mom. She has a lot to answer for."

I faced a similar situation with my daughter later on and handled it just as poorly as the girl's dad did. At the same time, my world was changing drastically. What's fair to men? In a troubled relationship or leaving one, without intimacy and sex for a long spell, are we bad guys for seeking other female companionship at the worst possible time for our children, spouses, friends and family? At times of separation or divorce, it seems the nature of the hunter works against us, and a lifetime building a good reputation can be gone before the dew dries on the rose.

Understanding how men are constructed by nature (chapter 2 and 3) helps to understand dad. Men invariably avoid intimate conversations about their girlfriends and spouses with other guys. That's private, maybe an ego thing. When intimacy is gone in a marriage, though, we seek another woman. Remember, for men, intimacy and sex are intertwined. We can't have one without eventually having the other.

PART 2 HAPPY GUYS   *14. Intimacy with Dads and Husbands*

 ***What Works for Guys***

- Support your hero.
- Encourage his intimacy and affection with the children, as well as your children's affection with dad. Show him how.

15. Becoming a Woman Who Makes a Man Happy

When you wish upon a star,
makes no difference who you are.
When you wish upon a star,
your dreams come true.
Walt Disney

When we focus on what can be, instead of wasting energy on what we don't like, we become creators. If you want to be a woman who makes men happy, try on the next three thoughts for size.

Attitude. In your bones you want to please your man. Tell it to the mirror until the refection believes you. When you know you can please him, that very attitude triggers the brain to adjust. Remember, the more you do something, the more cells the brain assigns to that task. Then picture male attributes you find attractive in your man or other men you know: he keeps his emotions in check so everyone else will stay calm. He asks questions and likes to play devil's advocate; he explores points of view. He's confident, and sometimes cocky. He communicates. He finds solutions to difficult situations, and, thank god, he makes "do you concur" eye contact with you as he organizes important decisions. He's a team player and refreshing straight-shooter about his thoughts. And how about the way he feels … you know—loving and enveloping when he hugs …

Visualize. Dale Carnegie said, "Picture in your mind the person you desire to be, and the thought you hold is hourly transforming you into that person." Alice Walker said something similar: "The present you are constructing should be the future you want to live." Visualization happens in the present and change in the future. Silicon Valley successes are a prime example of having created the future from the present. Ergo, visualize your attitude towards him, converting any negative energy to positive, and start the future now. You have just improved your chance for success immeasurably. Remember to smile.

Homework. Pick five phrases that describe what you want in your future. Then narrow the options to three. My initial five are the following:
1. a mellow satisfaction with life
2. a trusting, fun relationship with my wife
3. enough time with my children
4. a traveler's patience and curiosity
5. to be a writer on important issues and of children's stories

Now you try five!

My final three are:
1. a mellow satisfaction with life (gives me 3 and 4)
2. a trusting, fun relationship with my wife
3. to be a writer on important issues and of children's stories

Now you pick three. Repeat them every 24 hours until they're in your brain by rote.

Thoughts that come to my mind now:

Trust your man, but let him earn it. Things go wrong (money, arguments, etc.), so allow for being hurt sometimes knowing the risk is worth the reward.

Change, the hardest of all human endeavors. It means changing habits ingrained in us. Habits are comfortable. *But,* with a modicum of courage and real commitment, change is possible. **Hint:** Sometimes it's best to change location, which certainly takes courage.

Remember, anything you do often enough, you will learn to do well. When cells break down, they regenerate with updated information. So instead of looking for a magic potion, you can be busy experiencing.

Repeat this Mantra:
I trust (name);
I listen to him;
I support him.

16. All You Need Is Trust

Trust is the reason beautiful truth exists.
Trust is everything.

So now we've come to the end of the book and I'm thinking *all you need is trust, and the more you do something, the more cells the brain assigns to that task.* If you trust him, you listen. If you listen like Maslow, chances are you will understand his point of view, and that translates into a prime opportunity to resolve issues and make both of you happy.

Let's see how trust enhances time-honored cornerstones of relationships.
Respect: Many people are worthy of your respect. But it's one thing to respect someone, and quite another to trust them. Respect means you appreciate one or more fine qualities. Trust is deeper. When you trust someone, not only do you respect them, but you can also confide in them.
Truth: If truth is beauty, trust is its creator. You trust someone to hear your point of view. What's more gratifying than feeling heard?
Faithfullness: This is a fragile cornerstone of a long-term relationship in my mind, but if you remove your ego and trust enough to listen to the why of someone's unfaithfulness, you just might keep a relationship viable.
Love: With trust, you accept love's risks.
Friendship: Show me a good friendship; I will show you trust.
Soulmates: can you have a soulmate without trust? What would be the purpose?
Intimacy: Can you have intimacy without trust?

Empathy: A person can be empathetic without trust, but in a relationship with trust, empathy becomes intimacy.
Individual Growth: Trust is everything!

Trust Account

A good relationship is like a healthy bank account, only the currency is trust. If your balance is low and you want happiness, *make three deposits to each withdrawal.* Better yet make withdrawals anathema.

What is your balance?

Deposits:
- **the big ones** - trust and listening
- saying 3 positives to 1 negative daily. Positives: a big hello, small kindnesses, a smile or complement any time of day, Valentine's Day sex, telling him he is your hero (**double points**), doing things to please him even if you don't particularly like them (like visiting dull friends or watching a game with him), touching him (males need twice as much touch as females), complementing money-earned,
- asking dudes what they think
- informing him that you have an issue (see Chapter 11)
- sharing what's on your mind
- having your fights in bed, naked
- striving for a healthy self-esteem (a crucial component of happiness)
- honey-do lists and 80% rule

Withdrawals:
- arguments, character assassination
- not allowing complaints to be aired
- taboo topics (money, weight, need to be right)
- denying there is a problem
- bad-guy syndrome

What Works for Guys

**Keep a healthy balance
in your Trust Account with him.**

Summary of What Works for Guys: Chapters 7 - 16

- **Don't forget the spice.** Dress to thrill and be anthropologically kinky.
- **Insert romantic ideas into a "Romance Cheat Sheet"** in your phone. Plan ahead, set the mood, and Practice! Practice!
- **Trust him.**
- **Solve the problem.**
- **Cherish that one thing you love about him.**
- **You are who you were meant to be**, but you can adjust.
- **3 to 1 approach. Say 3 good things about him to every criticism.**
- **Support your hero.**
- **Encourage his intimacy and affection with the children.**
- **Mantra: I trust; I listen; I support**
- **Keep a healthy** balance in your Trust Account with him

For Further Reading

- Woman, Natalie Angier, Houghton Miffin, Co., 1999, USA
- Female Brain, Louann Brizendine, Broadway Books, New York, 2006, United States
- The Male Brain, Louann Brizendine, Random house books, New York 2010
- Sapiens, A Brief History of Humankind, Yuval Noah Harari, Vintage Books, Penguin, Random House, 2011, UK
- Sperm Are From Men, Eggs Are From Women, Joe Quirk, Orion Books LTD, 2007, London, Great Britain
- The Profit, Kahlil Gibran, UBS Publishers Distributors LTD., New Delhi, India, 1993 reprint
- How To Make A Woman Happy (A Guide For Men), Denis Hickey, Vingdinger Publishing LLC, 2014, USA
- Breaking Free, Denis Hickey, Vingdinger Publishing LLC, 2013, USA
- The Traveler, Denis Hickey, Vingdinger Publishing LLC, 2014, USA
- The Brass Verdict, Michael Connelly, Published by Little, Brown & Company, October 16th 2008, USA
- The Last Coyote, Michael Connelly, Published by Little, Brown and Company, 1995, USA
- Travels, Michael Crichton, Published by Valentine books, a division of Random House Inc., January 1993, USA
- 50 Shades of Gray, E L James, published by Vintage Books, 2011, USA

www.ingramcontent.com/pod-product-compliance
Lightning Source LLC
Chambersburg PA
CBHW050557300426
44112CB00013B/1952